Cambridge Elements

Elements in Reinventing Capitalism
edited by
Arie Y. Lewin
Duke University
Till Talaulicar
University of Erfurt

THE FUTURE OF WORK IN DIVERSE ECONOMIC SYSTEMS

The Varieties of Capitalism Perspective

Daniel Friel
University of San Andrés

CAMBRIDGE
UNIVERSITY PRESS

Shaftesbury Road, Cambridge CB2 8EA, United Kingdom

One Liberty Plaza, 20th Floor, New York, NY 10006, USA

477 Williamstown Road, Port Melbourne, VIC 3207, Australia

314–321, 3rd Floor, Plot 3, Splendor Forum, Jasola District Centre,
New Delhi – 110025, India

103 Penang Road, #05–06/07, Visioncrest Commercial, Singapore 238467

Cambridge University Press is part of Cambridge University Press & Assessment,
a department of the University of Cambridge.

We share the University's mission to contribute to society through the pursuit of
education, learning and research at the highest international levels of excellence.

www.cambridge.org
Information on this title: www.cambridge.org/9781009500210

DOI: 10.1017/9781009234627

First published 2024

A catalogue record for this publication is available from the British Library.

ISBN 978-1-009-50021-0 Hardback
ISBN 978-1-009-23460-3 Paperback
ISSN 2634-8950 (online)
ISSN 2634-8942 (print)

Cambridge University Press & Assessment has no responsibility for the persistence
or accuracy of URLs for external or third-party internet websites referred to in this
publication and does not guarantee that any content on such websites is, or will
remain, accurate or appropriate.

The Future of Work in Diverse Economic Systems

The Varieties of Capitalism Perspective

Elements in Reinventing Capitalism

DOI: 10.1017/9781009234627
First published online: January 2024

Daniel Friel
University of San Andrés

Author for correspondence: Daniel Friel, dfriel@udesa.edu.ar

Abstract: This Element reviews the varieties of capitalism approach (VoC) first developed by Hall and Soskice and subsequent extensions to emerging markets. The author suggests that by reinvigorating existing ideal types and creating new ones through an analysis of its five variables in a variety of countries VoC can be used to evaluate the viability of economic reforms across a wide range of countries. He argues that governments should base changes on lessons from other countries belonging to their ideal type. This Element illustrates the utility of VoC in understanding how reforms will differ across countries by examining how the future of work is likely to differ across nations depending on the degree to which the five institutions explored in this approach promote the standardization of tasks. It analyzes how these institutions shape degrees of standardization in the United States, Germany, and Brazil, offering suggestions for reforms in each of them.

Keywords: varieties of capitalism, comparative capitalism, comparative institutionalism, future of work, reforming capitalism

ISBNs: 9781009500210 (HB), 9781009234603 (PB), 9781009234627 (OC)
ISSNs: 2634-8950 (online), 2634-8942 (print)

Contents

1 Introduction

The increasing penetration of artificial intelligence (AI) and robotics into everyday workplaces has led to the proliferation of scenarios about the future of work ranging from utopic visions of shorter workweeks and higher incomes to declining wages and the practical enslavement of individuals to algorithms. Although concerns about the impact of new technological developments on jobs have existed since the Luddite movement in the early nineteenth century, Schwab (2017) argues that the emergence of these developments since the beginning of the twenty-first century adds new urgency to this debate. In the past they tended to affect one industry at a time, enabling people to shift to new jobs as their previous ones were eliminated. Today, the ability of displaced employees to find new jobs is cast in doubt by the fact that new developments are simultaneously disrupting almost every sector. Blue-collar jobs are being threatened by the introduction of increasingly sophisticated advanced manufacturing and automation, while white-collar ones are now being threatened by AI (Ford 2018). A particular challenge to these jobs is coming from generative AI programs such as ChatGPT. This type of software reduces the time dedicated to writing reports of all sorts by roughly 44 percent (Garg 2023). Improvements in robotics and AI enable firms to achieve the same output and higher quality with significantly fewer employees at almost all levels. They are also affecting professions ranging from factory workers and engineers to doctors and people employed in the entertainment industry. The current strikes by writers and actors in the United States over the ability of AI to write scripts and create virtual actors is just one indication of the extent to which AI in particular has changed industries that were once thought to be safe from automation.

There is a general feeling of discontentment across capitalist countries. Although new technological developments could potentially lead to a growing standard of living in which the demand for more leisure activities could create a variety of new jobs (Nübler 2018), most people in capitalist societies across the world currently do not share this optimistic outlook. A 2019 poll by Edelman Trust Barometer found that 58 percent of people across the globe believed that capitalism was doing more harm than good (McCarthy 2020). Individuals are increasingly feeling anxious about whether the existing rules of the game actually benefit the average person (Ford 2018). Social contracts are on the decline, while political discontent and polarization is growing (Paus 2018). In the United States, more than two-thirds of white working-class individuals believe that large corporations and the wealthy control elections (Case and Deaton 2020). Wolf (2023) contends that there is a growing sensation that neither capitalism nor democracy are serving people's interests. Significant portions of populations in democratic countries are losing faith in democratic institutions, causing the growth of right- and left-wing populist movements (Wolf 2023) that blame their feelings of malaise on immigrants or minorities (Ford 2018). Seventy-eight percent of the people in the United States that said their economic situation was worse in 2016 than in 2012 voted for Trump (Baldwin 2019). In Germany, the far-right AfD has become the second strongest political party after the Christian Democrats (Loveday and Brady 2023). "If business interests and the plutocracy become overwhelmingly powerful, democratic capitalism may fall apart, to be replaced by a plutocratic or autocratic version" (Wolf 2023: 318). Democratic countries are facing a situation similar to that of the 1930s and 1940s. Governments need to respond to these challenges by developing better policies in order to avoid the potential collapse of democracy (Wolf 2023).

The increasing unease of people in democracies is often link to the apparent ability of robotic automation such as advanced manufacturing and AI to eliminate jobs. Indeed, one report argues that job losses from new technological developments in OECD countries could be as high as 57 percent (Smith 2023). Nevertheless, another report claims that it could be as low as 9 percent (Chandy 2017). Those reports that have high estimates about the number of jobs that will be lost to these technologies do not make the distinction between the elimination of jobs and the replacement of tasks by automation (Smith 2023). Arntz, Gregory, and Zierahn (2016) contend that those studies that register higher numbers simply categorize entire jobs as being safe or possible to automate. They argue that researchers should consider that a job has the potential to be eliminated if 70 per cent of all tasks in it can be automated. Using this threshold, they contend that only 9 percent of individuals in the United States face a high likelihood of losing their jobs to new technological developments. Some countries have extensive craft sectors. Work in these fields will be more difficult to automate because tasks change often. Hence, fewer workers are likely to lose their jobs to AI and robots in these sectors. The prevalence of craft sectors and craft-style work in other areas can explain why despite the fact that Germany, Italy, South Korea, and Denmark had high growth rates in robot density between 1993 and 2007, they lost considerably fewer manufacturing jobs than the United Kingdom and the United States (Nübler 2018).

Job losses may also not impact all professions equally. Although Balliester and Elsheikhi (2018) claim that the destruction of old jobs will be greater than the creation of new ones, a survey of 18,000 employers from forty-three countries by Manpower group in 2017 found that 64 percent of firms believed that technology would not have an impact on the quantity of people they would employ over the next two years (World Bank 2018). The jobs most affected by

new technological developments are middle-skilled ones. Losses in these jobs could be more than compensated by an increase in the number of positions at the upper and lower ends of the job market (O'Reilly et al. 2018). These developments in the twenty-first century tend to augment the efficiency of workers by making some of the tasks they perform more efficient, not by replacing their jobs outright (Nübler 2018). Firms could actually maintain workers and implement new technologies if productivity improvements lead to an expansion of the breadth and/or depth of market penetration.

The technical possibility to use robots and AI rather than humans for the provision of certain tasks need not mean that the substitution of humans by "machines" actually takes place (Arntz, Gregory, and Zierahn 2016). Artificial intelligence and robotics need extensive standardization in order to prove effective (Autor et al. 2020). In order to determine the potential impact of these new technological developments on the future of work and the availability of jobs in a given country, we need to understand the degree to which tasks are standardized in it. A variety of factors, including batch sizes and/or inputs with varying quality, can limit the extent to which tasks in a country can be standardized and therefore the degree to which AI and robots can prove helpful; these factors are present in traditional industries as well as in services. Given the relationship between standardization and these developments, those countries with the highest level of standardization will also face the greatest political challenges in accommodating displaced workers. The degree to which tasks can be standardized is linked to the historical evolution of institutions in a given country, whereby the governments in those countries in which institutions support standardization will be more challenged to develop policies to mitigate the impact of new technological developments on individuals. This argument is illustrated in Figure 1.

Arntz et al. (2016) argue that legal, economic and social hurdles have a significant impact on the pace at which any country is being transformed by these new technological developments. How they will impact a given society is a political question (Paus 2018: 5). "The impact of technological change on the future of jobs is not deterministic, but is influenced by the capabilities that a society has accumulated through past experience, and by those it will develop in the future" (Nübler 2018: 64–65). The future of work in any country is not

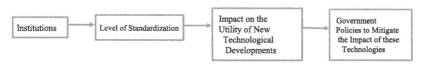

Figure 1 Illustration of my argument.

simply determined by technological developments. The prospect for the proliferation of good jobs on a massive scale depends on governmental policies (Nübler 2018). Polanyi (2001) contends that governments can either speed up or slow down the rate at which change occurs. He claims that the intervention of the Tutor and early Stuart governments in England were critical in slowing down the enclosure movement, thereby providing individuals time to find new jobs in the emerging cities. People need time to adjust to change.

Governments in emerging markets will not face the same pressure to change their policies as those in the developed world simply because technologies take time to spread throughout the world. The widespread adoption of any new technological developments on a grand scale often takes decades (Arnold et al. 2018; Atkinson 2018; Paus 2018). New technological developments from the last 20 years will take a significant amount of time to impact the majority of industries and workplaces (Atkinson 2018; Autor et al. 2020). Today, 17 percent of the global population still does not have electricity, while almost half of the world's inhabitants still does not have access to the Internet (Schwab 2017). Disruptions in labor markets caused by AI and robotics will impact emerging markets later than developed ones (Paus 2018). Nevertheless, there are also significant differences across these former countries that shape the impact of AI and robotics on the operations of firms. Although overall investments in AI in the world have increased by over 9,000 percent from 2010 until 2021, they have been concentrated in Europe, the United Kingdom, the United States and China. Private investments in AI in 2020 reached $23 billion in the United States and $9.9 billion in China (The Economist Group 2022). Although China now competes directly with advanced industrialized countries in a wide range of industries and has more multipurpose industrial robots than the United States, the majority of its producers only undertake extremely basic manufacturing activities. Except for a few large companies, most of the firms in China undertake little innovation and witness slow productivity growth.

In contrast to China, the majority of countries in Latin America and sub-Saharan Africa never created a significant number of labor-intensive manufacturing jobs (Paus 2018). This observation can explain why China has 49 robots per 10,000 workers, while this number is 16 in Argentina and 11 in Brazil (Oppenheimer 2019). While China is expected to see its GDP grow by 26.1 percent by 2030 as a result of the introduction of AI, it is predicted that Latin America will only see an increase in its GDP by 5.4 percent over this same period as a result of AI. This region simply does not have the existing talent needed to develop an effective AI ecosystem. Moreover, 41 percent of the population in Latin America did not even have access to the Internet in 2018

(The Economist Group 2022). Less than half of the population in this region have enough skills to use computers for basic operations. Consequently, it is not surprising that Latin America has lagged behind in the adoption of new technologies (Cadena, White, and Lamanna 2023).

Given the radical differences not only between Germany and the United States but also between China and the vast majority of other emerging market countries, scholars, and practitioners alike are in need of a theoretical framework that can enable them to understand the impact of new technological developments on the future of work in a given country and how governments could tailor policies to their local circumstances. Such a framework should use a set of critical factors to identify similarities between countries so that they could learn from each other. Copying policies from radically different countries would prove counterproductive as they would not address the specific problems facing a given country. Individual studies will not suffice as we need to be able to group countries according to their institutional similarities so that they can potentially learn from one another and avoid copying reforms from countries that have radically different circumstances. Wolf (2023) argues that any change in policy should be in accord with existing institutions. He analyzes a variety of institutions ranging from tax codes to government policies to promote innovation. Nevertheless, he does not provide an overarching theoretical framework for systematically comparing how existing policies and the changes needed differ between countries.

The field of comparative institutionalism provides the basis for effectively comparing countries. Within this area of research, scholars have focused on "the varieties of capitalism," developing a diversity of frameworks for understanding institutional differences across the world. This Element focuses on the most predominant one developed by Hall and Soskice (2001) entitled the varieties of capitalism (VoC) approach. I argue that VoC is better suited for making these comparisons than other theories in this field because it focuses on five critical institutions in capitalist societies, assigns countries to different ideal types and demonstrates how a particular combination of institutions shapes the competitiveness of firms in a given country. Although some of the existing ideal types need to be modified and others created, I argue that this approach encapsulates the most important variables shaping the strategies of firms. I maintain that this theory can prove particularly useful not only in helping scholars understand why the future of work will be different across countries but also in enabling governments to grasp the types of reforms they need to undertake to confront the specific challenges presented by new technologies.

In the next section, I summarize the evolution of institutional theory and its influence on VoC. It pays particular attention to how institutions in capitalist societies have evolved, highlighting the importance of path dependency. The following section describes the underlying concepts and logic of the VoC approach, paying particular attention to how this theory explains why companies from countries with different institutional structures can thrive in global competition. It also describes the major ideal types that have been developed using this approach. Section 4 examines the major competitors to VoC and evaluates the most important criticisms of this theory. It suggests that some existing ideal types need to be reenergized and new ones created by means of a fine-grained analysis of the five institutions of VoC in a variety of countries. In this section, I coin the term, non-standardized mass production, to describe the type of production most prevalent in emerging markets. The following section analyzes the future of work in capitalist societies, summarizing what type of work can be conducted by AI and robots and arguing that these new technological developments will have the greatest impact on those economies with the highest level of standardization. It includes an analysis of how the five institutions in the VoC framework will shape the impact of these developments in the United States, Germany, and Brazil; they were selected because they are exemplars of the three most developed ideal types in this approach. I argue that the United States will be more affected by new technological developments because business operations are more standardized in this country, while Germany and Brazil have specific, but different, mitigating factors. The next section examines how the ideal types developed in VoC can help policy makers design regulatory reforms to address the challenges of the future of work in these three countries. The conclusion presents a summary of the arguments made in this Element, while also providing guidelines for future research.

2 Institutional Theory and the Varieties of Capitalism Approach

At the heart of political economy lies a debate as to whether economic growth will improve the conditions of the poor. Scholars drawing on neoclassical economics contend that economies will grow faster and the conditions of everyone will improve if governments do not interfere in the operation of markets (Coates 2000). Countries supposedly can only reach a maximum level of growth by eliminating regulations (Elmslie and Criss 1999). Adam Smith contends, "had human institutions, therefore, never disturbed the natural course of things, the progressive wealth and increase of the towns would, in every political society, be consequential" (Smith 1776: 503). However, Smith also saw how regulations could benefit the functioning of markets. For example, he was in favor of laws that required inheritance to be divided among all children in a family because he believed it would improve the allocation of capital and lead to lower prices of property (Smith 1776). This insight opens up conversations about the proper role of regulation. Those scholars supporting statutory interventions point out that countries with a significant degree of regulation have reached levels of productivity and economic growth that are equal to more "liberal" ones (Hall 2015). Given this fact, it is not surprising that alternative capitalist paths have not only emerged but persisted (Storz et al. 2013). Convergence toward one liberal model of minimal government interference is simply not necessary for countries to prosper and even thrive.

The recognition of the fact that economies can persist without eliminating governmental regulations draws attention to the need for scholars to clearly understand how institutions emerge and evolve. North (1990) examined how institutions provide the basis for efficient interactions by providing actors sets of incentives and disincentives to behave in particular ways. The institutions he examines range from regulations that are enforced by laws to informal practices that generate expectations about how people should conduct themselves. Institutions act as "collectively enforced expectations" that generate predictable patterns of behavior (Streeck and Thelen 2005). They establish the basic rules of the game and improve the efficiency of human interactions by reducing uncertainty (North 1990). "The idea of persistence of some kind is virtually built into the very definition of an institution" (Mahoney and Thelen 2010: 4). Institutions improve the efficiency of organizations by allowing parties to transactions to avoid having to explain their perceptions and understandings to each other, thereby enabling them to coordinate their activities without centralization. (Streeck and Thelen 2005). Actors resist changing institutions because the efficiency of their operations is derived from existing ones (Deeg and Jackson 2008). Neoclassical economists and those scholars that draw inspiration from this school of thought do not neglect the impact that institutions have on the behavior of actors. "However, they tend to neglect the effects that institutions can have on the strategic interaction between actors – that is, those effects that are stressed by those who favor the varieties of capitalism framework" (Allen 2004: 98).

Institutions arise out of individuals sharing common historical experiences that in turn form common expectations across society. Coordination between actors is also facilitated by shared histories and consistent expectations (Paul 1994). "The more actors adopt and apply a specific institution (i.e., an organizational rule or routine), the more efficient the interaction among these actors is, since the behavior of the actors is rule guided and can therefore be anticipated and reactions can be considered in advance" (Sydow, Schreyögg, and Koch 2009: 699). As actors continue to behave in ways in accordance with existing institutions, they constrain human behavior and provide a sense of consistency within a society (David 1994). Repeated behaviors create path-dependent ways of acting in an economy. Present decisions are shaped by how actors within a society are expected to behave. Yet, they are potentially unaware of how institutions shape their behavior (Arthur 1994; David 1985). A certain degree of obedience is a precondition for coordination in and outside organizations. This obedience reinforces the value of institutions creating lock-ins (Sydow et al. 2009) in which actors are often unable to change their behavior even in the face of more efficient options (Arthur 1989).

One of the most significant differences in theories about institutions revolves around whether they are consciously designed by humans rationally weighing costs and benefits (North 1990) or emerge out of a country's history and culture (Powell and DiMaggio 1991). Rational choice institutionalism is a theory based on the premise that institutions arise from utilitarian calculations. This form of institutionalism presupposes that actors have fixed preferences that they seek to maximize through rational action (Schmidt 2010). It assumes that individuals work together to create institutions to realize mutual benefits. A particular institution endures because it provides more benefits than alternatives. Since humans construct institutions, they can decide whether or not to obey them (Hall and Taylor 1996). The literature on rational choice institutionalism overlooks how historical contexts shape human behavior (Jackson et al. 2019). By contrast, historical institutionalism examines how institutions arise from historically contingent social compromises (Streeck 2001; Streeck and Yamamura 2003; Thelen, 2004; Thelen and Steinmo, 1992), while sociological institutionalism probes how individual preferences arise from cultural contexts. It attributes variations in behavior across societies to differences in rules and norms (Schmidt 2010). Historical institutionalism and sociological institutionalism focus on how human behavior is shaped by factors beyond their control. Actors are even sometimes unaware of how history and culture shape their behavior (Thelen and Steinmo 1992).

The repetition of behavioral patterns creates path dependency in a society, causing the institutions of the past to shape future ones (David 1994). Some scholars argue that institutions shape the way people interpret the behavior of others and even what they can imagine themselves doing. These scholars argue that they even shape how individuals frame solutions to problems (Hall and Taylor 1996). These existing patterns of behavior shape the nature of institutions that actors will design for new circumstances (Hall and Taylor 1996; Sydow et al. 2009). New institutions cannot simply be grafted onto existing political economies without being shaped by existing ones (Hall and Thelen 2009). Institutional slates can neither be simply wiped clean nor ignored (Fligstein and Freeland 1995; Jackson and Deeg 2006; Thelen and Steinmo 1992). At the same time, any evaluation of the efficiency of institutions has to take the context in which action occurs into consideration. A particular type of action is only efficient in a given context. What is efficient, depends on the context. One society may be more efficient than another not because it has the right set of institutions but rather because its institutions create stronger lock-ins, thereby ensuring that behavior lives up to expectations. At the same time, attempts to simply copy institutions between countries without probing their degrees of institutional similarities could prove counterproductive if the two countries involved don't have relatively similar institutions.

Nevertheless, Streeck and Thelen (2005) contend that actors do not respond to incentives provided by institutions in a mechanistic fashion. Instead, they switch from one to another as it suits their purposes. Their ability to change their behavior, and potentially institutions themselves, results from their capability to exploit tensions between institutions (Deeg and Jackson 2007). Friedland and Alford (1991) argue that humans and organizations achieve autonomy by exploiting contradictions between institutions such as the Christian religion, the nuclear family and the bureaucratic state. Giddens (1984) contends that traditional theory in Sociology "exaggerates the degree to which normative obligations are 'internalized' by the members of societies" (30). It fails to recognize humans as knowledgeable agents. For Giddens (1984) scholars should examine the interaction of action and structure instead of assuming that structure determines action. Actors draw on the resources and rules in social systems, while also using their knowledge and understanding to alter their behavior.

It is possible to envision action as being embedded in structure even while claiming that social context is shape by the actions of individuals. "In contrast to many economic theories, practices are not viewed as detached from but as socially embedded in contexts" (Sydow and Windeler 2020: 270). Granovetter (1985) argues that theories in Sociology generally adapt either oversocialized or undersocialized approaches, whereby the former assumes that structure determines action and the latter presumes that structure has no impact on agency. Granovetter (1985) promotes an embedded approach which recognizes the importance of structure without assuming that it determines action. Nevertheless, as mentioned above, the efficiency of organizations and societies more generally depend on the ability of individuals to coordinate their activities with others. Even if a particular actor wishes to change an institution or adapt a new one, such an act only proves beneficial if others also adapt this change. Otherwise, coordination proves more difficult and efficiency declines. At the same time, radical change would prove impossible if institutions do indeed shape how we interpret our surroundings.

Whether an individual can truly act in a manner that is not in accord with his or her institutional setting depends on the type of institutions that he or she is challenging. Williamson (2000) argues that there are four different levels of institutions. Lower levels have a limited influence on those immediately above them, whereas upper levels impose clear limits on lower ones. The highest, and most general, level is what he terms embeddedness. Institutions at this level are informal and consist of customs, traditions, norms, religion, etc. They are slow to change and "have a lasting grip on the way a society conducts itself" (Williamson 2000: 597). The second level, the institutional environment, consists of formal rules such as constitutions and laws. They emerge partially out of an evolutionary process and partially out of design. Barring an exogenous crisis, change usually takes centuries. At the third level, namely governance, actors seek to reduce conflicts and bring about mutual benefits through the adaptation of complex contracts or agreements. If complexity cannot be reduced, cooperation for mutual benefit does not occur. The fourth level is resource allocation. It is the level of the production function for companies. It incorporates the institutions that guide the operation of an organization, whereas the governance level describes institutions governing relationships between organizations (Williamson 2000).

Williamson (2000) argues that scholars often do not describe the level of institutions they study. Although he does not discuss the implications of this oversight, arguably much of the confusion between, and sometimes within, disciplines in the social sciences regarding the degree to which actors can alter institutions result from scholars studying institutions at different levels, while believing they are studying the same phenomena. Those studying institutions at the level of embeddedness are more likely to attribute less agency to actors, while those examining them at the level of resource allocation are likely to see actors as having more agency. For those that study the levels of governance and resource allocation change is easier, while for those studying the other two levels it is more difficult. Work focusing on the latter two levels tends to overlook the impact of the former on the behavior of individuals. Rational choice institutionalism focuses on the levels of governance and resource allocation, while historical and sociological institutionalism concentrates on embeddedness and formal rules. The work of Giddens (1984) discusses agency at the lower two levels, while examining how institutions at the higher ones influence the decisions of actors. What remains unclear is how institutions at these two higher levels shape those at the lower ones. For example, labor market institutions at these higher levels clearly shape how a particular manager forms institutions at the level of resource allocation when he or she hires someone. At the same time, these two upper levels clearly have an impact on the strategies firms pursue.

Work in comparative institutionalism and comparative capitalism more generally focuses on the levels of embeddedness and formal rules in Williamson's framework. Unlike neoclassical economics, scholars using these frameworks do not assume that one set of institutions is naturally superior to any other. Instead, they presume that a variety of institutional settings can lead to similar levels of profit and social well-being (Hotho and Saka-Helmhout 2017). Work in both of these fields pays particular attention to how interrelationships between institutions shape not only the resources available to firms but also the type of organizations they are likely to develop. Hence, they can explain why similar industries across nations are organized in strikingly different manners (Jackson and Deeg 2008a). Albert (1993) was the first scholar to contrast what he termed were Neo-American and Rhine models of capitalism. The former is focused on individual achievements and short-term profits, while the latter is rooted in collective achievements and consensus among economic actors. He believed that these two economic systems were in a struggle that would eventually be won by the Neo-American model. By contrast, Streeck (1991, 1996, 1997) was more optimistic about the survival of the Rhine model of capitalism. He contended that a set of seemingly anti-capitalist institutions arising out of historical struggles in Germany provided that economy with the means to survive global competition.

Streeck's arguments (1991, 1996, 1997) are based on an earlier work by Sorge and Streeck (1988) in which they describe diversified quality production. It is a means of modular production in which firms realize a flexible combination of standardized components into a wide variety of different products. They demonstrate that this form of production is "supported by a 'virtuous circle' of mutually reinforcing 'deviant' features of the German version of capitalism, such as strong trade unions, institutionalized worker participation on the shop floor and above, high wages with low wage spread, high employer investment in workforce skills and high employment security" (Streeck 2010: 14). Sorge and Streeck (1988) demonstrate how a set of institutions that seemingly undermine the efficiency of a capitalist economy can actually sustain particular forms of production and enable firms to be competitive on world markets. Their work demonstrates why countries do not have to converge toward a liberal model. Although some adaptations were made to economic regulations in Germany since the emergence of diversified quality production, this basic institutional structure has remained intact (Sorge and Streeck 2018). Sorge and Streeck (1988) were the first scholars in this field to identify a clear set of variables shaping firm behavior within the comparative capitalism framework. Yet, they did not examine these variables in other countries. As we will see in the next section, Hall and Soskice (2001) build on their insights by developing the VoC approach. It provides the basis for probing the extent to which other institutional configurations could also prove effective in enabling firms to compete on global markets.

3 The Theory underlying VoC and Its Application across the World

The VoC approach is considered to be not only the most important theory in the field of comparative capitalism (Crouch 2005; Jackson and Deeg 2012; Nölke and Vliegenthart 2009; Nölke et al. 2020; Peck and Theodore 2007), but also the most comprehensive one for studying capitalist economies (Buhr and Frankenberger 2014). It has shifted attention in political economy away from traditional topics such as inflation and unemployment (Baccaro and Pontusson 2018), toward an understanding of how a specific set of social and economic institutions shape the strategies of firms. VoC seeks to promote "a firm-centered political economy that regards companies as the crucial actors in a capitalist economy," drawing particular attention to how firms solve coordination problems with an extensive range of actors (Hall and Soskice 2001: 6). Yet, it does not attribute economic growth to the unbridled agency of firms. Instead, it seeks to understand how national institutions shape their potential success in the global economy. By demonstrating how two different sets of institutions enable firms to develop equally successful strategies, it challenges standard conceptions of globalization that assume that economies will have to converge toward one institutional model (Baccaro and Pontusson 2018; Peck and Theodore 2007; Thelen 2012). Peck and Zhang (2013) contend that while scholars have heavily criticized VoC over the years, "it is nevertheless the case that its stylized models of CME and LME systems have been remarkably provocative and potent, earning an important place in mainstream political-economic imaginaries" (362). This section summarizes the main tenants of this approach before describing how it has been used to examine institutional structures across the world.

3.1 The Theoretical Framework

Unlike other theories in comparative capitalism, VoC focuses on a narrow set of five institutions that arguably capture the most important areas of coordination in an economy (Thelen 2012). Specifically, it examines how institutions in the spheres of corporate governance, industrial relations, vocational training and education, inter-firm relations and employee relations shape the strategies of firms (Hall and Soskice 2001). Although the term corporate governance is customarily used to describe the manner in which major decisions are made in a corporation, Hall and Soskice (2001) use it largely to represent how firms finance their operations. The term industrial relations designates how collective bargaining occurs between firms and their workers. The sphere of vocational training and education concentrates on how firms are able to access workers with the skills they need. Inter-firm relations is the sphere used to describe the relationships that firms have with their suppliers, other companies and clients. This theory also includes the sphere of employee relations. It covers those institutions that firms need to coordinate activities with their employees (Hall and Soskice 2001). I have argued elsewhere that this sphere should include labor laws (Friel 2011).

In some countries these institutions form complementarities. "Two institutions can be said to be complementary if the presence (or efficiency) of one increases the returns (or efficiency) of the other" (Hall and Soskice 2001: 17).[1] Complementarities exist when institutions enhance each other's benefits (Crouch et al. 2005). For example, the presence of works councils in Germany provides employees the job security they need in order to be willing to learn company-specific skills (Allen 2004). Hall and Soskice (2001) examine complementarities only between the five institutions outlined above. These complementarities are critical for economic growth because they provide firms comparative institutional advantages that enable them to compete effectively on global markets. Such an advantage enables a firm to produce certain types of goods more efficiently than others due to the institutional support provided by their home country. This concept enables scholars to understand why companies in the same industry in different countries react differently to the same exogenous pressures (Jackson and Deeg 2006, 2008a). Hall and Soskice (2001) directly link the economic performance of an economy to the existence of complementarities and their corresponding compara-tive institutional advantages. Given the advantages firms can draw from compara-tive institutional advantages, "companies *can be expected* [emphasis added] to gravitate toward strategies that take advantage of these opportunities. In short, there are important respects in which strategy follows structure" (Hall and Soskice 2001: 15). Nevertheless, Hall and Soskice (2001) only identify two types of comparative institutional advantages. Each of them is linked to one of the two ideal types identified in their approach.

3.2 VoC in the Developed World

The two ideal types developed by Hall and Soskice (2001) are liberal market economies (LMEs) and coordinated market economies (CMEs). Germany is considered the quintessential CME, while the United States is the prime

---

[1] By contrast, this term is used by some scholars to describe how one institution can compensate for another (Deeg 2005).

example of an LME. These ideal types are simultaneously its greatest appeal and the source of much of its criticism. Although VoC is predominantly focused on countries in the North Atlantic (Peck and Theodore 2007), Hall and Soskice (2001) briefly describe a third ideal type that they label Mediterranean. Molina and Rhodes (2007) call these countries mixed market economies and argue that they are typified by Italy and Spain. Unlike LMEs and CMEs, this ideal type does not have complementarities or a comparative institutional advantage. Its sphere of governance resembles that of CMEs while its labor relations are similar to those in LMEs. Schmidt (2003) contends that the omnipresent role of the state in economies such as France, justifies the inclusion of a new ideal type that she labels state capitalism. She argues that large, state-sponsored projects in areas such as telecommunications, electricity, transport and aerospace have enabled firms to perform well in these industries. Yet, according to the analysis of Hall and Soskice (2001) countries like Italy, Spain and France do not possess a comparative institutional advantage. Therefore, they would apparently be ineffective at competing on global markets. As we will see below, this is also the case for some ideal types develop using VoC to describe countries in emerging markets.

3.2.1 Liberal Market Economies

In LMEs, coordination between economic actors occurs primarily through markets or hierarchies (Hall and Soskice 2001). The institutional structure of LMEs fosters short-term horizons in the area of corporate governance, minimal employee representation in industrial relations, on-the-job training in the area of vocational training and education, competitive relations between firms in inter-firm relations and near unilateral managerial control in employee relations (Soskice 1999). In the sphere of governance, the preference of short-term over long-term gains leads companies to be reluctant to make long-term investments in research and development. This short-term orientation also causes firms to eschew long-term relations with suppliers and rely principally on arms-length market relations to structure its interactions with them. The preference for markets also predominates in the area of vocational training and education. Workers are expected to obtain the education they need for a particular job. The focus on short-term gains also causes firms to resist unionization and to pursue strategies that are built around the ability to easily hire and fire workers. At the same time, fluid labor markets also cause employees to focus more on their careers than the success of the firm. Flexible labor markets enable firms to easily hire personnel to make entirely new products. Firms can easily find the employees they need and quickly dispose of them if a project proves unprofitable.

At the same time, limited restrictions on mergers and acquisitions enables companies to easily obtain the new resources they need for novel projects. Management is also not limited by unions in making decisions to pursue the production of radically different products. These attributes of LMEs provide them a comparative institutional advantage in radical innovation.

The most significant drawback of this ideal type is the fact that it is "institutionally light" (Hay 2020), characterizing countries by the institutions they lack (Thelen 2001). In the end, the LME ideal type "is a curious hybrid of neoclassical economic theory and a correspondingly idealized form of American capitalism" (Peck and Theodore 2007: 751). By constructing the LME ideal type in this manner, VoC risks repeating the mistake of orthodox economics of reifying the US capitalist system by simply assuming that textbook descriptions of how economies should work actually describe this economic system. In doing so, it perpetuates the assumption that some markets are less embedded than others (Peck and Theodore 2007) and ignores how the nature of institutions in countries resembling this ideal type actually shape the strategies of firms. I have shown elsewhere how the apparently "liberal" institutional context in the United States limited the ability of a German firm to implement a lean production program at one of its facilities in that host country (Friel 2003, 2005). In terms of inter-firm relations, Chandler (1977) argues that the Sherman Act, legislation designed to limit the formation of trusts, "discouraged the continuation of loose horizontal federations of small manufacturing enterprises," thereby hastening mergers between companies (375).

3.2.2 Coordinated Market Economies

Coordination between economic actors in CMEs takes place largely through non-market institutions that facilitate deliberation. The institutional structure of this ideal type promotes long-term horizons in corporate governance, employee representation in the area of industrial relations, cooperation between firms, governments and employees in the area of vocational training and education, collaboration between firms in inter-firm relations and tempered managerial control in employee relations (Soskice 1999). Firms in CMEs rely on extensive relational contracting based on exchanges of information within networks that privilege collaboration over competition. In terms of governance firms are willing to make long-term investments as they emphasize long-term over short-term gains. This orientation permeates the relations firms have with suppliers, causing them to prefer working with the same supplier rather than searching for new ones on the market. The close relationship between firms and their suppliers encourages mutual help in improving products and production processes.

Industrial relations are extensively coordinated with works councils actively participating in a consensus decision-making process at the highest levels of the firm. In terms of vocational training and education companies typically coordinate it through apprenticeships that provide workers with industry-specific instead of task-specific skills. These skills prove critical in enabling workers to shift production to new products within the same general industry. Firms are not afraid to train workers in these skills because strong labor laws and unions limit employee turnover and provide a basis for workers to be committed to their employer. These institutions provide firms a comparative institutional advantage generating incremental innovations. "The workforce (extending all the way down to the shop floor) is skilled enough to come up with such innovations, secure enough to risk suggesting changes to products or process that might alter their job situation, and endowed with enough work autonomy to see these kinds of improvements as a dimension of their job" (Hall and Soskice 2001: 39).

Despite the specific descriptions of institutions in CMEs, this ideal type is often used as a simple repository for economies that do not meet what Hall and Soskice consider to be the US standard (Peck and Theodore 2007). Some scholars have even used this ideal type to describe Japan and northern European countries, despite the significant differences that these economies have with the description of a CME (Streeck and Yamamura 2003). Fligstein and Zhang (2011) contend that China is a peculiar type of CME that is closer to France than the United States, despite the fact that Hall and Soskice (2001) do not consider France to be a CME. Indeed, they consider France to belong to the Mediterranean ideal type. To a certain extent, this type of confusion is to be expected, because it is impossible to fit all political economies of the world into one of these categories without overstretching them (Feldmann 2019). It is important to assign a given economy to one of these ideal types because the failure to do so would lead to the conclusion that it did not have a comparative institutional advantage. Therefore, any potential success could not be explained using the VoC framework.

3.3 VoC in Emerging Markets

Given that VoC was originally designed to describe capitalist economies only in the developed world (Bohle and Greskovits 2012; Jackson and Deeg 2019), some scholars doubt its utility for analyzing countries outside the OECD (Jackson and Deeg 2019). Storz et al. (2013) contend that it is misguided to construct theories about capitalism based solely on evidence from Western countries. Given its origins, it is not surprising that scholars that use VoC to describe institutional structures in emerging markets treat these countries as "idiosyncratic deviations from an ideal historical standard" that have irrational, incoherent, and dysfunctional structures (Wehr 2015: 142). Yet, such characterizations cannot explain why between 1990 and 2010 the portion of world GDP attributed to the United States, Great Britain, Germany, and Japan declined, while that of Brazil, China, and India doubled (Nölke et al. 2015). As it currently stands, this theory cannot account for the fact that emerging market countries have outperformed developed ones. The theory developed in VoC is complicated by the fact that state-led economies in emerging markets have been growing more than liberal ones. (Nölke et al. 2020). If VoC is to prove relevant for analyzing institutional structures in emerging markets, it arguably will have to abandon its contention that economic growth occurs only in those economies that resemble LMEs or CMEs (Nölke et al. 2020; Wehr 2015). This section explores what new ideal types within VoC have been developed to explain the institutional structures of emerging markets. Schedelik et al. (2021) identify four such alternative ideal types: hierarchical market economies, dependent market economies, state-permeated economies, and patrimonial market economies. Each one of them will be discussed in turn before I turn to an analysis of how VoC has also been used to analyze Asian countries.

3.3.1 Latin America

Schneider (2009, 2013) developed the hierarchical market economy (HME) ideal type to describe the institutional structure of Latin American economies. He uses the term hierarchy to emphasize the resolution of coordination problems through the firm instead of through markets as occurs in LMEs or through cooperation between firms as happens in CMEs.[2] Schneider (2013) argues that institutions in Latin America are largely weak or missing. Hierarchical market economies rely largely on self-financing because high levels of political and economic uncertainty cause firms to shun using the stock market. Unions in Latin America are also considered weak. They have little influence on the shop-room floor and are not involved in the training of workers. Firms in general are not interested in pursuing forms of production that require high-skilled workers because employee turnover is high and few workers complete secondary education.[3] Weak contract enforcement in these countries complicates the ability of firms to rely on suppliers, causing them often to pursue vertical

---

[2] Here it should be noted that technically the LME ideal type also contemplates some coordination through hierarchies.

[3] Morgan, Doening, and Gomes (2021) argue that this turnover is augmented by a large number of informal workers that do not have incentives to improve their skills.

integration instead of contracting suppliers. Employee relations in HMEs are atomized as workers tend not to stay long at any one particular job. Schneider (2009) argues that although labor laws in Latin America are tougher than those in the United States, they are rarely enforced.[4]

Schneider (2013) argues that HMEs have negative complementarities. They are even worse than no complementarities at all. At the same time, they are strong enough to prevent these economies from converging toward LMEs or CMEs. Apparently, firms from HMEs would seem to perform worse on world markets than even those firms from countries that do not have any complementarities. In a similar vein, Wood and Schnyder (2021) argue that VoC should include a theory about comparative disadvantages. Nölke et al. (2020) argue that the HME model is widely criticized for relying on modernization theory. The introduction of the concept of comparative disadvantages and negative complementarities only reinforces this bias causing scholars to believe that these economies have no choice other than to merge toward a LME or a CME. Nevertheless, Schneider (2009) contends that even the liberalization policies of the 1990s did not alter the basic institutional structure of these economies. They would seem to have no hope of improving. Moreover, the HME model has been faulted for failing to capture the institutional diversity in Latin America (Ebenau 2015; Schedelik et al. 2021) and the differing degrees to which governments in this region are involved in their economies (Ebenau 2015).

3.3.2 Eastern Europe

A number of scholars contend that the traditional VoC framework does not adequately capture the unique features of capitalism in East Central Europe (Bohle and Greskovitis 2009, 2012; Nölke and Vliegenthart 2009). They date back to an era in which these countries had communist governments (Bohle and Greskovitis 2009; Stark 1996). Social ties and even organizational forms that existed during this period became resources once a capitalist system began to emerge (Stark 1996). For example, Nölke and Vliegenthart (2009) contend that the socialist educational system was basically preserved in East Central European countries. Although Feldmann (2007) argues that the traditional ideal types associated with VoC are useful in explaining capitalist institutions in Estonia and Slovenia, Nölke and Vliegenthart (2009) propose another ideal

---

[4] Kiran (2018) argues that Turkey is also an HME. As in Latin America, Turkey has diversified business groups, a low-skilled workforce and a weak industrial relations system. The unions that do exist in Turkey, like those in Latin America, often seek the patronage of political parties and occasionally the state itself.

type that they believe is more adequate in capturing the institutional structure of capitalist systems in four other East Central European countries. The work of the latter is addressed before turning to the former.

The most influential model for East Central European countries is the one developed by Nölke and Vliegenthart (2009). They coin the ideal type dependent market economy (DME) to describe the institutional configuration in Hungary, Poland, Slovakia, and the Czech Republic. They incorporate the areas of finance, corporate governance, industrial relations, education, and the manner in which innovations are undertaken into their model. Unlike LMEs and CMEs, DMEs are fundamentally dependent on multinational corporations. Foreign companies account for almost half of the gross domestic product of the Czech Republic, Hungary, and Slovakia. They also are responsible for roughly one-third of it in Poland. Moreover, 80 percent of assets in the banking sector are controlled by foreign companies (Šćepanović and Bohle 2018). National business groups are largely absent (Nölke et al. 2020).[5] As far as industrial relations is concerned, collective bargaining coverage is higher than in LMEs but lower than in CMEs. Workers technically have representation on the advisory boards of corporations but in practice they do not influence the behavior of firms. Training occurs largely within public institutions and without the participation of companies. As regards innovation, DMEs are largely imitative, relying occasionally on incremental innovation and issuing few patents (Nölke and Vliegenthart 2009). It is important to highlight that the DME ideal type does not include two of the original variables of VoC, namely inter-firm and employee relations. Perhaps, the most controversial part of this ideal type is the inclusion of the topic innovation. In the original VoC framework the type of innovation in an economy is a result of complementarities of other institutions.

Although Hall and Soskice (2001) describe how institutional complementarities arise from the five variables contained in their approach, Nölke and Vliegenthart (2009) examine how they are formed from the variables of labor, finance and innovation. They contend that complementarities formed from innovation and finance from abroad combined with local skilled labor provide firms a competitive advantage in the production of semi-standardized industrial goods and the assembly of relatively complex and durable consumer ones. Despite the fact that these authors argue that complementarities should be a critical component for scholars using VoC, they do not utilize this concept in the manner outlined by Hall and Soskice (2001). In its original conception,

---

[5] In order to emphasize the importance of foreign companies in these economies, Myant and Drahokoupil (2010) have argued that they should be considered foreign direct investment-based economies.

complementarities were seen as arising only out of national institutions. The only national institution examined by Nölke and Vliegenthart (2009) is worker skills. The other two variables, namely capital and innovation, come from the headquarters of multinationals outside of these countries. Skills alone cannot provide firms a comparative institutional advantage. In contrast to Nölke and Vliegenthart (2009), Bohle and Greskovits (2012) contend that DMNEs are a form of HME that has multinational companies instead of business groups.

Although Feldmann (2019) agrees with Nölke and Vliegenthart (2009) that the traditional ideal types developed by Hall and Soskice are not useful for understanding the vast majority of countries in East Central Europe, he argues that the LME ideal type captures the institutional structure of Estonia, while the CME model proves useful for understanding it in Slovenia. In making this argument, he carefully examines the five institutions in the original VoC approach in each of these countries. He contends that differences in the privatization process in Slovenia and Estonia shaped the future of governance in them. In the former old networks of owners persisted, while in the latter companies were privatized to outsiders. Although stock market capitalization was higher in Estonia than in Slovenia, in both countries they are rather underdeveloped. In terms of industrial relations, Slovenia has a unionization rate of 42 percent and the most extensive system of collective bargaining in East Central Europe. It also has legally mandated works councils with an option for firms to have worker representatives on management boards; under communism the former state of Yugoslavia, of which Slovenia was a part, had works councils and worker self-management. By contrast, in Estonia the unionization rate is 14 percent and collective bargaining agreements have very low coverage. Furthermore, co-determination does not exist. The educational system in Estonia focuses on general skills, while the one in Slovenia provides workers firm-specific ones based on traineeships. As far as inter-firm relations is concerned, firms in Slovenia are required to be members of the chamber of commerce, while coordination between firms in Estonia is limited. Feldmann (2019) explores the topic of employee relations by examining the flexibility of labor markets, arguing that these markets in Estonia are more adaptable than those in Slovenia. Average job tenure in Slovenia is 12.1 years, while it is 6.9 years in Estonia. Although Felmann's descriptions of these countries imply that Slovenia would have the comparative institutional advantage of a CME and that Estonia would have that of an LME, he does not explicitly explore this topic. Yet, such an analysis is critical for any study using VoC.

3.3.3 State-Permeated Economies

Nölke et al. (2015) created the state-permeated market economy (SME) ideal type to describe the institutional structures in Brazil, China, and India. "In simple terms, SMEs are less dependent than DMEs, less liberal than LMEs and less coordinated than CMEs" (8). China is the most typical case of an SME, while Brazil has some characteristics of a more liberal model. According to these authors, the economic growth of these countries along with their importance for the global economy calls into question the need for these countries to converge toward another ideal type. Echoing criticisms of VoC in the developed world, they argue that this framework does not pay enough attention to the role of the state in shaping these economies. Governments in SMEs help firms in ways ranging from direct control of educational institutions to assistance for technological upgrading (Nölke et al. 2020). Although SMEs are said to be rather weak in regulating their economies, this "limited central state power is indeed compensated by strong, multilayered and reliable interpersonal public-private relations at different levels" (Nölke et al. 2020: 193). This cooperation generally does not occur through formal business associations. Consequently, these interactions are fragmented but dynamic, while also being subject to accusations of corruption (Nölke et al. 2020). Building on the work of Nölke and Vliegenthart (2009) on dependent market economies, Nölke et al. (2015) only examine the first three institutional spheres in the VoC approach, namely governance, labor relations as well as vocational training and education. Like the previous work, they also incorporate innovation as one of the institutional spheres to be studied. Each of these institutions in SMEs is discussed in turn.

In terms of governance, Nölke et al. (2015) point out that enterprises owned directly by the state contribute 30 percent of the GDP in Brazil and 29.7 percent in China. Even after a wave of privatization in India in the early 1990s, over 70 percent of the most important companies remained family-owned. Corporate control continues to be dominated by insiders. Possible takeovers are practically impossible in China not only because many of them are owned by the government but also because two-thirds of the shares of any company generally cannot be traded. These firms rely for 82.9 percent of their funds from banks, while the stock market accounted for only 9 percent of them. At the same time, 75 percent of all firms in China were privately held in 2007 (Witt and Redding 2014). Musacchio and Lazzarini (2014) point out that although most large Brazilian companies are listed on the stock market in that country, family shareholders or other block holders practically prevent companies from being taken over. Even as governments in SMEs reduce their holdings of shares in companies, they continue to have influence over them by providing sources of financing. Large firms in these countries tend to rely on their own profits and government subsidized loans to finance their operations (Nölke et al. 2020). Nölke et al. (2015) highlight that on average 50 percent of national banking assets are possessed by governments in SMEs. In the end, most bank loans are in reality credit lines provided by the state, often through development banks. The quantity of these loans is significant. For example, the Brazilian Development Bank lends four times as much money as the World Bank, or roughly 7.5 percent of this country's GDP (Nölke et al. 2015). Such loans have lower interest rates and longer maturity periods than those that can be obtained on the open market. By offering firms these loans, governments cannot only align the goals of national companies with their own, but also ensure that they are less reliant on foreign capital. Consequently, foreign direct investment plays only a minor role in these economies (Nölke et al. 2020).

Labor relations in SMEs are regulated at the firm level, thereby undermining the bargaining power of workers. Effective trilateral collective bargaining bodies are absent and attempts to incorporate workers into the decision-making processes of firms have largely failed. Moreover, the state is often unwilling to enforce laws that favor unions (Nölke et al. 2015). Although the union density rate in China is over 40 percent, they are inherently tied to the state and have little real independence. Unionization rates in Germany and India are similar. However, their collective bargaining power in India is more limited (Nölke et al. 2020). Sometimes unions have practically no power even when they are not dependent on a government. For example, unions in Brazil often have little power to shape even wage rates (Friel and de Villechenon 2018). Greater unionization in SMEs is limited by the fact that labor markets are segmented into a relatively small but well-paid and well-protected segment of workers and those that work in a low-cost, often informal, segment (Nölke et al. 2020). State-permeated market economies have vocational training systems that provide the vast majority of industrial workers with a secondary education. However, the quality of it they receive lags behind what similar workers obtain in LMEs. Although governments are willing to invest in upgrading the skills of workers after they graduate, the demand for such workers is limited in SMEs. The innovation that does occur is largely limited to incremental changes applied to existing products. "Research and development expenditures are lower for SMEs when compared to CMEs and LMEs, but higher than in DMEs" (Nölke et al. 2020: 190).

Although Nölke et al. (2015, 2020) clearly show the importance of the state in the area of governance, they do not demonstrate why it is important for the other three variables they examine. In labor relations, except for the case of China, the state appears to have no role in shaping the dynamic between workers and owners. Its role in training seems to be similar to what is found in LMEs. Fligstein and Zhang (2011) contend that the Chinese government still has an important presence in almost every aspect of its economy. At the same time, it is unclear why Nölke et al. (2015, 2020) included innovation as a variable. As mentioned above, in the original VoC framework it is an outcome, not a cause. It is also not clear why these authors did not include inter-firm relations as one of their variables. Khanna and Palepu (1997, 2010) highlight the importance of challenges firms face when working with suppliers in emerging markets. In a similar vein, Schneider (2009, 2013) demonstrates how weak supplier markets cause firms to rely on vertical integration in Latin America. Both of these sets of authors show that diversified business groups in emerging markets are a direct response to weak institutions in inter-firm relations. Finally, it is unclear why Nölke et al. (2015, 2020) did not include an analysis of employee relations. The manner in which these relations are structured has a significant impact on the strategies of firms and their performance. Although Nölke et al. (2020) claim that SMEs have a comparative institutional advantage for producing middle-range products for domestic markets, they do not elaborate on how this advantage is formed. Furthermore, it is important to highlight that VoC was developed to explain how firms from a variety of institutional settings can be successful on global markets, not on their domestic ones.

3.3.4 Patrimonial Economies

Some authors have suggested the term patrimonial market economy (PME) to describe the institutional structure of Russia and Arab countries (Becker 2013; Becker and Vasileva 2017; Buhr and Frankenberger 2014; Schlumberger 2008). These economies are characterized as having strong patron-client relations uniting economic and political elites for purposes of rent seeking, cronyism and corruption (Becker 2013; Becker and Vasileva 2017). Relations between firms and governments are built on interpersonal trust created over years of interactions. Sometimes they are rooted in close personal relations or familial ties (Buhr and Frankenberger 2014).

In his analysis of PMEs in Arab countries, Schlumberger (2008) argues that there is a clash of formal and informal rules in which the latter usually prevail. He highlights the lack of laws protecting private property and competition as well as the absence of the rule of law more generally. In Saudi Arabia, the government functions as the principle economic actor, controlling financial institutions and crude oil producers. Unlike in DMEs, transnational capital plays little role in Arab countries. These economies are relatively isolated, relying primarily on locally owned manufacturers. Important sectors of production are still dominated by state-owned enterprises. The military also often owns a number of companies. Arab countries have the lowest level of manufacturing exports to GDP as well as the lowest share of private investment in its economy as a percentage of all forms of finance. Similar to CMEs, employees enjoy a high level of job security. Employee turnover is also normally low. The government plays an active role not only in regulating and subsidizing companies but also as an employer. It also retains significant stakes in banks. Through its interventions, these governments create a clear distinction between insiders who enjoy the benefits of having relations with the state and outsiders that do not. While those individuals that work for the state enjoy welfare benefits, they are customarily denied to others (Hertog 2022). King (2007) argues that patron-client relationships also pervade the Russian economy. He points out that ten business groups account for 50 percent of its economic output. Schneider (2013) contends that the Russian government dominates the most important economic activities in this country, enabling it to limit the emergence of large, independent businesses. Nevertheless, he argues that "Russia and some of the other former Soviet Republics seemed to be moving toward hierarchical capitalism" (30). Although the PME category is not directly related to VoC, scholars studying these economies could benefit from undertaking analysis of how the institutions identified in this approach shape the operations of businesses in these countries. Even if corruption pervades much of the activities in them, firms still need to coordinate their actions with workers, suppliers and other stakeholders.

3.3.5 Asian Economies

Based on a cluster analysis of thirteen countries in Asia, Witt and Redding (2013) contend that the CME-LME dichotomy only helps scholars understand portions of the Japanese economy. They argue that its utility is limited for describing other economies in Asia. To facilitate a better understanding of these economies these authors propose five new ideal types, namely emerging Southeast Asian, post-socialist, advanced city, advanced Northeast Asian and Japanese. They argue that "in a majority of Asian economies, the acquisition of professional skills is left to private initiative" (277). In terms of labor relations, they claim that, with the exception of China, Laos, and Vietnam, company unions dominate. While business groups provide their own sources of financing, other companies in Asia generally rely on banks. In terms of inter-firm relations, companies are found to lack institutionalized long-term cooperative ties with their suppliers. Personalistic ties permeate all parts of these economies, including relations with suppliers. Nevertheless, Witt and Redding (2013) do not show how these institutions differ in each of their ideal types, preferring instead to make generalizations that would appear to be more in line with one ideal type.

As we will see in the next section, the methodology of ideal types does not require real world cases to have all of the attributes of the ideal type proposed to describe them (Becker 2007; Crouch 2005; Hay 2020).

In contrast to Witt and Redding (2013), Schneider (2013) proposes network market economies (NMEs) as a singular ideal type to describe Asian economies. NMEs are characterized by long-term, non-contractual, non-market relations of trust and reciprocity as well as informal norms. Coordination in these economies occurs largely through informal networks that stretch across firms and sectors. In some NMEs, these networks include employees, government agencies, banks and even competitors. Relations with suppliers are also often long term. Similar to CMEs, NMEs have long-term employment relations. Schneider (2013) argues that some industrial economies in Asia have institutional structures that lie between NMEs and CMEs, while others are closer to HMEs. Future work on Asia could explore the extent to which individual economies in this region actually have characteristics of NMEs by examining in further detail the five institutions outlined in the original VoC approach. Scholars could also examine the type of comparative institutional advantages firms could derive from the institutional configurations of their home countries, while also probing whether other ideal types may better describe some countries in this region.

4 Criticisms of VoC and Competing Theories

In the previous chapter, I discussed how well the ideal types developed to describe a variety of countries have applied the concepts of VoC. By contrast, this chapter focuses on general criticisms of this approach, before analyzing how alternative theories address these concerns. It will also point out the limitations of these works. This chapter ends by suggesting how VoC can be improved based on the analysis herein.

4.1 Criticisms of VoC

The following section addresses the major shortcomings in VoC. These issues include the way it formulates and deploys ideal types, the need to include more variables, the limitations of the way in which it conceived complementarities and comparative institutional advantages, its inability to explain institutional change and the lack of firm agency. Each of these topics is addressed in turn.

4.1.1 The Use of Ideal Types

The VoC approach is often criticized for creating only two ideal types and placing them at opposite poles along a one-dimensional continuum and arguing that the only comparative institutional advantages available to firms exist at either of these extremities (Ebenau 2015; Ebenau et al. 2015; Hay 2020; Jackson and Deeg 2012; Molina and Rhodes 2007; Peck and Theodore 2007; Streeck 2010). The contention of Hall and Soskice (2001) that countries that do not resemble LMEs or CMEs should converge toward one of these ideal types resembles some of the basic tenants of modernization theory. Yet, VoC was supposedly developed in part to address problems with this theory. Ebenau (2015) argues that even proponents of this approach understand the need for it to better appreciate the diversity of potential advantages available to firms.

At the same time, Hall and Soskice (2001) confuse their ideal types with descriptions of ideal types (Becker 2007; Crouch 2005). Although they argue that Germany is a quintessential CME and the United States an exemplar of an LME, their descriptions of these ideal types are essentially accounts of these countries. Max Weber warned scholars to be aware of the possibility of making this mistake (Hay 2020). Ideal types are an heuristic tool used to sharpen comparisons across cases. There is no expectation that they will actually correspond to real cases (Dallmayr and McCarthy 1977). Ideal types are no more than stylized accounts designed to capture the essence of a phenomena. They intentionally accentuate some aspects of a phenomena and overlook others (Crouch 2005). In the end, "Capitalisms do not really come in varieties, even if it is sometimes useful to proceed on the basis that they do" (Hay 2020: 314). Becker (2007) argues that all cases contain elements from different ideal types. Consequently, it is "an empirical challenge to assess just how closely a particular economy comes to a given ideal type at a particular moment and whether there is change over time" (Feldmann 2019: 168).

Comparisons between ideal types using the VoC framework are hindered by the fact that scholars using it do not describe all of the five institutional variables in this approach for the ideal types they develop. Even when they do research these five variables, they do not use a common set of terms to describe them. This problem derives partially from the fact that Hall and Soskice (2001) used binary terms to describe these five variables. See Table 1 for a description of the difference of the ideal types discussed in the previous section.

4.1.2 The Need to Include More Variables

Hancké, Rhode, and Thatcher (2007) contend that VoC scholars could improve their understanding of the impact of institutions on the strategies of firms by relaxing its key premises and introducing more variables. It has been criticized for failing to include variables such as the welfare state (Jackson and Deeg 2006; Molina and Rhodes 2007), electoral systems, public policy and even macroeconomic policies (Nölke and Claar 2013). Other scholars have argued that VoC should include topics such as class (Bruff, Ebenau, and May 2015) and the world

Table 1 Differences between ideal types.

	Governance	Industrial Relations	Vocational Training and Education	Inter-firm Relations	Employee Relations
LME	Short-term	Minimal employee representation	On-the-job	Market	Unilateral managerial control & weak labor laws
CME	Long-term	Extensive employee representation	Coordinated between all actors	Long-term relationships	Coordination and commitment between workers and firms
HME	Self-financing	Minimal employee representation	Minimal training of workers with minimal skills	Vertical integration	Atomized relations with employees
DME	Comes from Multinational	Comes from Multinational	Extensive training	Not discussed	Not discussed
SME	Importance of state ownership	Regulated at the firm level	Minimal training of workers with minimal skills	Not discussed	Not discussed
PME	Role of state-controlled banks	Not discussed	Not discussed	Not discussed	High level of job security
NME	Role of banks	Company unions	Not discussed	Long-term relationships	Paternalistic relations

capitalist system (Ebenau 2015; Feldmann 2019; Wehr 2015). Some scholars in the field of comparative capitalism criticize VoC for neglecting the impact of the power of the state on firm behavior (Bohle and Greskovits 2012; Feldmann 2019; Molina and Rhodes 2007; Schmidt 2003; Tate 2001). Nevertheless, no theory can ever fully capture the potential impact that all variables have on a phenomena. Including more variables into the VoC approach would stretch it beyond its original purpose, making comparisons between countries more difficult. It does not seek to be an all-encompassing theory about capitalist economies. Its scope is restricted to seeing how a limited set of institutions shape how firms coordinate their activities with other actors and how the strategies of firms are related to the institutional settings in which they operate.

Some of the works on VoC in emerging markets discussed in the previous chapter have criticized it for failing to capture the unique features of economies outside of the developed world (Bohle and Greskovitis 2009, 2012; Nölke and Vliegenthart 2009; Nölke et al. 2015; 2020). Yet, none of these authors make this claim after having actually examined the five existing spheres of institutions in VoC. Only Feldmann (2019), Schneider (2013), and Witt and Redding (2013) examine all of the five of them in the countries they study. Although countries in emerging markets indeed have radically different institutions than the ones that exist in the developed world, scholars need to develop a framework that can be used to adequately compare and contrast countries across the world. It has to focus on a limited number of variables and I contend that those identified by VoC are the most critical in shaping the strategies of firms.

4.1.3 Problems with Complementarities and Comparative Institutional Advantage

One of the most important claims of VoC is that the institutional structures of CMEs provide firms in countries resembling this ideal type a comparative institutional advantage that enables them to develop strategies to effectively compete with LMEs. Hall and Gingerich (2009) probe the relationship between complementarities and rates of growth in OECD countries. They find not only that this relationship is statistically significant but also that the strategies of firms vary depending on the type of institutional support provided. Although Witt and Jackson (2016) confirm that complementarities in CMEs benefit firms pursuing incremental innovations, they also find that institutional complementarities in LMEs do not provide firms pursuing radical innovation any advantage. Indeed, firms pursuing this type of innovation in LMEs are shown to benefit from having institutions from opposing institutional logics rather than from complementarities.

Nevertheless, the work of Hall and Soskice (2001) is silent about potential sources of comparative institutional advantages in countries that do not have institutional complementarities associated with either of their ideal types (Jackson and Deeg 2012). According to Hall and Soskice (2001) Mediterranean economies do not have competitive institutional advantages because they do not have complementarities. They have liberal institutions in the area of industrial relations and non-market forms of coordination in the sphere of governance. According to the original theory developed by these authors, the countries that fit the Mediterranean ideal type, and the vast majority of the rest of the economies throughout the world, will have to converge toward either a CME or LME ideal type in order to benefit from a comparative institutional advantage. Nevertheless, Hall and Soskice (2001) cannot explain why some of these countries have been able to thrive in global competition without having such an advantage. Nölke and Vliegenthart (2009) are the only scholars that have articulated a new comparative institutional advantage enabling firms to compete on global markets. However, this advantage is constructed using only one of the five institutions in the original VoC approach. Hence, it does not construct complementarities and comparative institutional advantages in the manner imagined by Hall and Soskice (2001). Although some countries may indeed rely extensively on multinationals to compensate for missing institutions as claimed by Nölke and Vliegenthart (2009),[6] work still needs to be done to describe comparative institutional advantages for countries in emerging markets in a way that builds on the theoretical constructs of VoC.

The VoC approach has also been criticized for failing to consider that not all firms benefit from the institutional setting described in its ideal types (Bruff et al. 2015). For example, some sectors in Germany are simply not impacted by works councils and collective bargaining agreements (Allen 2004). Complementarities also appear to benefit only large companies and/or small firms in some industries (Deeg 2005). Moreover, the strategies of firms even within the same industry in the same country often differ. Jackson and Deeg (2006) argue that firms are able to pursue strategies that do not fit the institutional context in which they operate, while Friel and Teipen (2000) contend that any country has path-immanent and path-challenging strategies. Although firms are more likely to be successful if they pursue the former strategy, companies undertaking the latter type can also flourish.

---

[6] I would like to thank Martin Myant for helping me think through this point.

4.1.4 The Lack of Firm Agency

By attributing successful strategies of firms to comparative institutional advantages, VoC underestimates the role of agency despite the fact that Hall and Soskice (2001) contend that it is a firm-centered approach. By linking the strategies of firms directly to institutional complementarities and comparative institutional advantages, this theory seems to leave little room for agency. Firms are seen as choosing to adapt certain strategies even while they are also seen as having little other logical choice (Streeck 2010). In short, companies are considered "institution takers" and not autonomous actors (Deeg and Jackson 2007). VoC cannot explain why a firm would not fully embrace a strategy that is in accord with the institutional context in which it operates. At the heart of VoC is the assumption that the more firms align their strategies with existing institutions, the more successful they will be. As discussed in chapter 2, the efficiency of a firm depends partially on its ability to work within an existing institutional framework. This capability is critical because it enables firms to coordinate their activities effectively with actors both inside and outside its boundaries. Hall and Soskice (2001) contend that shared understandings "reduce the uncertainty actors have about the behavior of others and allow them to make credible commitments to each other" (10). As noted in chapter 2 repeated historical experiences serve to create a common set of expectations that facilitate coordination between actors. They cannot be simply changed or ignored at the whim of an actor. In this sense, Hall and Soskice (2001) argue that "firms located within any political economy face a set of coordinating institutions whose character is *not fully* [emphasis added] under their control" (15).

Several years after this approach was created scholars using it embraced the idea of considering institutions as resources (Deeg and Jackson 2007; Hall and Thelen 2009).[7] In doing so, they were arguably attempting to introduce ideas of agency into this theory, while also underplaying the constraints institutions impose on firms. However, it is unclear that this manner of conceiving institutions upholds the essence of the theory developed by Hall and Soskice (2001). Conceiving institutions as resources does not capture how they limit firm behavior. Some institutions can simply not be ignored. Moreover, given the nature of informal institutions, firms may not even be aware of the reasons why they embrace a certain strategy. Company executives may believe their choices are free of the influence of

---

[7] This conceptualization of institutions was also largely embraced in comparative capitalism (Deeg and Jackson 2007; Hotho and Saka-Helmhout 2017; Jackson and Deeg 2006, 2008; Peck and Theodore 2007; Streeck and Thelen 2005).

institutions, even if they are not. The idea of considering institutions as resources also implies that executives could choose not to use any of the resources provided to them by society. It is unclear if this is desirable even if it were possible.

In the end, executives have to choose between existing institutions. However, the institutions on which they can draw could be much broader than the dominant national institutions described by Hall and Soskice (2001). According to Hay (2020), they overlook sources of endogenous tensions, stress, and contradictions within an economy. Real economies, in contrast to ideal types, have institutional tensions as well as complementarities (Crouch and Farrell 2002; Deeg and Jackson 2007). Schneiberg (2007) argues that economies "are embedded within a broader institutional context populated by multiple logics, paths and principles" (51). Firms can take advantage of incoherence within institutional structures to form a variety of strategies (Crouch and Farrell 2002). VoC, and comparative institutionalism more generally, have practically overlooked how firms can creatively combine institutions to create of variety of strategies within a given context (Hotho and Saka-Helmhout 2017).

4.1.5 Problems Dealing with Institutional Change

Some scholars (Allen 2004; Streeck 2010; Thelen 2004) argue that functionalism is a central feature of VoC. By focusing solely on the function that these institutions serve, Hall and Soskice (2001) are said to overlook critical aspects about how conflict and power shape the evolution of institutions. Hall and Thelen (2009) argue that "The varieties of capitalism approach offers fresh and intriguing insights into differences among the developed economies, but it can hardly be considered viable if it cannot also comprehend processes of institutional change" (8). Hall and Thelen (2009) argue that over time institutions become fragile when they stop serving the interests of actors, leading to institutional change. According to Thelen (2004) this change does not have to be abrupt or obvious. Rather, it often occurs during periods of stasis marked by periodic renegotiations and realignments in political coalitions. According to historical institutionalists, relations between social groups are often tentative and marked by conflicts, causing institutions to be more or less in a state of persistent evolution. New institutions arising from the conflicts suspend but do not abolish them (Thelen 2004; Thelen and Steinmo 1992).

Some scholars contend that a liberalization process is undermining the distinction between liberal and coordinated market economies. Although a wide spectrum of reforms, ranging from the decentralization of collective bargaining agreements to corporate privatizations, are considered part of this process, "the crudeness of this category obscures more than it clarifies" (Hall and Thelen 2009: 22). Indeed, this way of characterizing reforms in general conceals the actual impact that they have on the behavior of firms. Even after extended periods of so-called liberal reforms, there are still substantive differences between coordinated and liberal market economies (Hall and Thelen 2009). Hence, it is possible for VoC to be revised to include an understanding of institutional reform without relinquishing its most important insights. VoC reminds scholars that conflicts are strongly influenced by the nature of existing institutions. Actors actually judge reforms based on how they interact with these institutions. In this context it is mistaken to view changes in institutions as a signal of alternations in the very manner in which activities are coordinated in a society. That said, institutions can only persist if they are adapted to change in the market and political context. Reforms are actually necessary to sustain a particular type of coordination (Hall and Thelen 2009). Indeed, Hall and Soskice (2001) support this understanding of institutional change. They contend that institutions should be expected to evolve to remain effective. Moreover, they argue that "our approach contains a number of conceptual tools for understanding both the nature of contemporary challenges and the shape this evolution is likely to take" (54).

4.2 Theories that Compete with VoC

There is no agreement in the literature about the number of distinct types of capitalisms or the variables that should be used to describe them (Jackson and Deeg 2006). However, there are three major frameworks in the field of comparative capitalism that represent viable alternatives to the VoC approach developed by Hall and Soskice (2001). They are the governance approach, national business systems and social systems of innovation (Jackson and Deeg 2012).[8] I will address each of them in turn.

The governance approach seeks to understand how "the totality of institutional arrangements – including rules and rule-making agents – that regulate transactions inside and across the boundaries of an economic system" shape economic behavior (Hollingsworth and Streeck 1994: 5). Unlike VoC, it is a loosely integrated approach that incorporates an understanding of how communities, networks, associations and government institutions at local and national levels shape firm behavior. In contrast to VoC, the governance approach contemplates the possibility that countries can have more than one

---

[8] For an excellent review of different approaches within comparative capitalism, see Crouch (2005).

model for coordinating activities within their boundaries, even while recognizing that one model is likely to be predominant (Jackson and Deeg 2008b). Using this approach, Locke (1995) and Regini (1997) examine how local and regional political networks in Italy provide firms a variety of resources and constraints, arguing that the lack of a coherent national economic system makes these institutions play an important role in shaping firm behavior. Sabel and Zeitlin (1997) demonstrate how municipal governments and employer associations help industrial districts in Northern Italy balance competition and cooperation. Often companies in these districts produce their own final products, while also making inputs for other members in them. Herrigel (1996) points out that similar networks are also found in Southwestern Germany. Although studies of regional forms of production help scholars understand the variety of institutions that can potentially impact the strategies of firms, Turner (1991) questions the importance of these institutions and forms of production in the vast majority of countries. He points out that almost all of the examples used to illustrate this type of regional governance are from Northern Italy. The fact that scholars using this approach draw on theories ranging from transaction costs to institutional legitimacy (Fligstein and Freeland 1995), undermines its potential utility for comparative work across countries. Hall (1999) argues that a major drawback of this theory is its attempt to be all-encompassing. He contends that scholars would be better served focusing on how a limited number of variables shape firm behavior.

Another major framework in the field of comparative capitalism is the national business systems approach created by Whitley (1999). Similar to scholars using the governance approach, he acknowledges that the predominant institutional configurations in a country help some sectors more than others. In contrast to Hall and Soskice (2001) and work using the governance approach, he specifically examines how his model can explain the structure of capitalist economies in Eastern Europe and Asia. Whitley (1999) identifies six models of capitalist countries: fragmented, coordinated industrial district, compartmentalized, state-organized, collaborative, and highly coordinated. These categories are created by identifying different ways in which activities are coordinated between owners, workers and other firms. These business systems are compared along the dimensions of means of ownership control, the extent of vertical integration, the extent of co-ownership in industrial sectors, the extent of collaboration between competitors, the degree of alliances within sectors, the degree of employer–employee interdependence, and the extent to which employees are given power. The key institutional variables that Whitley attempts to integrate into his model are the financial system, the skill development system, labor relations as well as trust and authority relations. Unlike VoC, this approach also integrates the role of the state into its models, considering how "the character of the state determines the degree of institutional coherence and homogeneity in firm behavior across the national economy" (Jackson and Deeg 2008b: 687). One of the most significant advantages of the national business systems approach is the fact that it does not measure capitalist diversity by the extent to which a country deviates from the Anglo-American norm (Jackson and Deeg 2006). However, the nature of these variables in any society is presumed rather than proven. Amable (2003) argues that "it is hard to find, in the book's claim, reflective and studiously non-judgmental elaborations of institutional combinations and mutations (or), any proposition that one could possibly disagree with or know how to set about testing for falsifiability" (9–10).

The social systems of innovation is another important approach within comparative capitalism. It is derived from regulation theory. It creates five models by examining in the following areas: product-markets competition, labor market institutions, finance, governance, education, and the welfare state. It delineates five models, namely market-based, socio-democratic, Continental Europe, Mediterranean, and Asian. Although the Continental European model possesses features similar to that of the social-democratic one, it has a higher degree of employment protection and a welfare state that is less developed. The Mediterranean model has more employment protection but less social protection than the Continental one. The Asian model lacks state-sponsored social protections and employment protection is provided by firms (Amable 2003). There is also a degree of overlap between Continental European, Mediterranean, and socio-democratic models. The most significant limitation of this theory is the fact that it basically categorizes countries according to regions. Although it is laudable for including Asian countries, it completely overlooks Latin America and some regions in Europe. According to Jackson and Deeg (2006), this model synthesizes many aspects of VoC, while being sensitive to social embeddedness. Peck and Theodore (2007) contend that this approach's most significant weakness is that it lacks parsimony, thereby limiting its ability to effectively compare countries.

4.3 Where to Go from Here

The majority of work using VoC to generate new ideal types has focused on regions. Although the social systems of innovation has explored differences between institutional settings in Europe, it has not been applied to countries outside this region. By contrast, the national business systems approach has shown differences within regions in Europe and Asia. Making such distinctions is critical because countries can be dramatically different from one another even in the same region (Lewin and Kim 2004). For example, together with a colleague I have shown that there are significant differences in labor laws and union power between Argentina and Brazil (Friel and de Villechenon 2018). Instead of focusing on the details of how a particular institution in a given country functions, work using VoC commonly focuses on ad hoc descriptions of institutions that emphasize their economic functions (Jackson and Deeg 2006). As mentioned in Chapter 3, work still needs to be done to document the details of institutions in LMEs. Indeed such work could actually lead to a rethinking of the role institutions play resembling this ideal type. Consequently, scholars should be leery about relying on broad categories to create testable propositions (Hay 2020). According to Feldmann (2019) "Disagreements about categorizing key cases across different frameworks suggest that more research is necessary before we achieve anything approximating a tentative consensus on classifying capitalist systems on a global scale, which is why more comparative analysis of economic governance across multiple institutional fields is an important task for future research" (189). Only research based on a fine-grained analysis of the five institutions in VoC will enable scholars to appropriately assign a country to its most relevant ideal type.

After such research is undertaken, scholars are likely to begin to identify new patterns that could lead to the formation of new ideal types or the revision of existing ones. In conducting such research the work of Witt et al. (2018) should prove particularly useful because it creates a plethora of different ideal types that encompass the sixty-one major countries that account for 93.5 percent of global GDP. Scholars can build on it by exploring the five institutions of VoC in-depth in each of these countries. Work in the area of the social systems of production could also help scholars using VoC to potentially create new ideal types for many of the countries that are now considered to be CMEs. In examining the potential for new ideal types, the work of Witt and Jackson (2016) may also prove particularly helpful because they sketch five potential ideal types. However, until now they have only been used to provide a basic description of different institutional structures in Asia. Researchers could explore whether other countries throughout the world have similar institutional settings. Although scholars should not be afraid of developing new ideal types, they should avoid creating ones that just describe one country such as the one Witt and Jackson (2016) created for Japan. Comparisons across countries are best done between broad categories of countries. As I will demonstrate in Section 6, countries that are close to the same ideal type could learn from each other how to better reform their institutional settings.

Echoing concerns of scholars using the national business system approach, others within the field of comparative capitalism criticize VoC for neglecting the impact of the power of the state on firm behavior (Bohle and Greskovits 2012; Feldmann 2019; Molina and Rhodes 2007; Schmidt 2003; Tate 2001).

Nevertheless, Hall and Soskice (2001) contend that its role in shaping firm behavior is evident in all five institutional spheres of their approach. Banking laws underlie corporate governance. A series of regulations shape industrial relations. Training systems are structured by government regulations. Contract and anti-monopoly laws guide inter-firm relations. In addition, a series of labor laws and regulations shape employee relations. A similar argument is made about the failure of theories like VoC to contemplate the role of a variety of institutions in emerging markets. Maira and Martib (2009) argue that even though emerging markets may lack the formal institutions commonly found in the developed world, they have a plethora of other ones that significantly affect how business is conducted in these countries. Although this is an important insight, VoC does not need to add new variables in order to accommodate it. Instead, scholars using it need to examine its five institutional spheres at different levels. Although Hall and Soskice (2001) maintain that national institutions have the greatest impact on corporate strategy, they also say "that differences in corporate strategy can be conditioned by the institutional support available to firms at the regional or sectoral levels" (15). Given that the original theory developed by Hall and Soskice (2001) did not contemplate institutional structures in emerging markets, scholars should not draw the conclusion that national institutions are more important than those at regional or sectoral levels in shaping the strategies of firms in these countries. At the same time, Allen (2004) points out that VoC presumes that institutions are universally spread across a country. In areas and regions even in the developed world in which one or more of the five national institutions examined in VoC is not relevant, scholars should document the nature of the particular institution(s) at the state or local level.

People do not live without institutions in any part of the world. However, they may be found at a variety of levels. The work of Williamson (2000) provides a means for extending the work of the study of the five institutional spheres of VoC to three new levels. One of the most daunting tasks facing scholars using VoC is understanding how level one institutions in Williamson's (2000) framework, namely informal institutions and shared understandings, shape the strategies of firms. Differences in these institutions are even evident in the distinctive ways in which the same term can be interpreted differently at the level of employee relations. In an analysis I conducted at a German multinational implementing a lean production program in the United States and Germany, I found that quality control managers had radically different understandings of teamwork. This manager at the German facility defined teamwork as "the active participation of employees, including those on the shop-room floor, in designing methods for completing tasks as well as discovering and solving problems" (Friel 2003: 240). By contrast, this manager at this firm's US facility contended that teamwork involved setting common goals and values as well as enhancing the flow of information (Friel 2003). Although extending the levels at which the variables in VoC are examined would enrich our understanding of the impact of institutions on firm behavior, it would also make cross national, and even national, comparisons more difficult even if it would still remain focused on a limited number of variables.

Nevertheless, work on the five institutional variables of VoC at the levels described by Williamson (2000) as well as those at the state and local level could potentially help scholars to discover comparative institutional advantages for ideal types besides CMEs and LMEs. Such advantages could be formed from the same five spheres of institutions, albeit at different levels. In conducting such research, scholars could build on an article in which I argue that firms can draw on past and present institutions to form their own comparative institutional advantages (Friel 2011). In forming such an advantage companies could potentially draw on the four levels of institutions describe by Williamson (2000) as well as on state and local ones. Firms in emerging markets would seem particularly prone to form comparative institutional advantages in this manner because national institutions are often weak or missing according to Khanna and Palepu (1997). Such work may also be a promising way of introducing more agency into the VoC framework. Indeed, even companies in the developed world may also form comparative institutional advantages in a similar manner.

At the same time, in order to fully appreciate the ramifications of VoC for understanding how institutions shape the strategies of firms and their comparative institutional advantages, it is necessary to expand the implications of this theory beyond the topics of radical and incremental innovation. These concepts seem to have been deployed by Hall and Soskice (2001) only as a means for describing how companies develop products. However, it is also critical to understand how they produce them. Arguably, companies located in LMEs would prefer mass production because workers have limited or task-specific skills. The lack of unions combined with weak labor laws and low levels of worker commitment also favor this form of production. Hall and Soskice (2001) specifically mention that CMEs are particularly well suited to diversified quality production. Citing Streek (1991), they point out that this type of production is based on "strong trade unions, institutionalized worker participation on the shop floor and above, high wages with a low wage spread, high employer investment in workforce skills, and high employment security" (14). However, they do not mention that this form of production customarily involves the creation of a wide variety of products in relatively small batches. I argue that HMEs have a comparative institutional advantage in the production of medium and low quality goods. Yet, I contend that firms in these countries do not produce goods in a mass standardized way. Instead, I coin the term non-standardized mass production to describe how production occurs. It is indeed mass production because companies generally produce large quantity of goods. However, problems in receiving quality, standardized goods from their suppliers limit the ability of firms to standardize their own operations. The manner in which institutions create the basis for this type of production is discussed in the following two chapters. After describing the general impact of artificial intelligence and robotics on the future of work in general, the next section demonstrates why these new technological developments have the greatest impact on LMEs. Then, Section 6 demonstrates why governments seeking to reform their economies to confront the challenges resulting from the introduction of these new technological developments should learn from countries that belong to their same ideal type.

5 The Future of Work

The VoC approach has demonstrated that persistent differences in institutional structures across countries continue to shape the strategies of firms. Hall and Soskice (2001) contend that these differences will also shape how firms react to the appearance of new technologies. Yet, they do not elaborate on this claim. I will do so in this chapter. I argue that the degree to which a country will be affected by AI and robotics will be shaped by the extent to which the five variables in VoC favor the standardization of production processes.[9] First I will turn to a brief description of how the nature of work in general has changed before analyzing how VoC can help scholars understand the future of work in the United States, Germany, and Brazil. As mentioned in Section 1, these three countries were chosen because they are exemplars of the most consolidated ideal types, namely LMEs, CMEs, and HMEs, respectively.[10]

5.1 The Increasing Impact of AI and Robots

According to Schwab (2017), a radical disruption in the nature of work began to take hold with the advent of the third industrial revolution in the 1960s. It started with the introduction of semiconductors and mainframe computers. The rise of personal computers in the 1970s and the Internet in the 1990s intensified this

---

[9] Here it should be noted that standardization does not apply just to manufacturing. Even service industries are subject to it.

[10] I would like to thank an anonymous reviewer for helping me to properly focus the analysis in this section as well as the following one.

change. Schwab (2017) argues that a fourth industrial revolution began to take hold in the beginning of the twenty-first century with the emergence of artificial intelligence, nanotechnology, and biotechnology. Nevertheless, O'Reilly et al. (2018) cast doubt on the revolutionary nature of these changes, arguing that they were merely improvements on earlier developments.

The most important technological developments are occurring in the areas of robotics and AI. Yet, both of these technologies are like any other tool. Although robots and AI perform complex tasks and may seem to act autonomously, they are still applying the rules provided to them by humans (Malone 2020). Algorithms principally perform classification and prediction functions based on the instructions they are provided (Zamora 2020). The real value of computers is their speed and accuracy in accomplishing these tasks (Canals 2020; Kalleberg 2018). The value of any computer program is limited if the data it processes differs substantively from what was used to write it (Gil et al. 2020). Until now these programs are only good at recognizing patterns, not determining cause and effect (Canals 2020). Artificial intelligence still has limited capacity to complete even simple tasks such as monitoring content and categorizing data. It has proven effective at artificial narrow intelligence, namely the ability to perform a specific task. However, it has been unable to achieve artificial general intelligence, that is to say reasoning and problem-solving capabilities (Berg et al. 2018).

Artificial intelligence faces significant difficulties undertaking tasks that require information from a disparate set of examples. While they need a large quantity of examples in order to identify new objects, children only need a few (Gil et al. 2020). Humans are still needed to process different kinds of information and perform complex tasks (Kalleberg 2018). "The ability to adapt to entirely novel situations remains an enormous challenge for AI and robotics, a key reason for companies' continued reliance on human workers for a variety of tasks" (Autor et al. 2020: 34). Tacit knowledge presents a particular challenge for artificial intelligence (Johannessen 2018). "There are many tasks that people understand tacitly and accomplish effortlessly but for which neither computer programmers nor anyone else can enunciate the explicit 'rules' or procedures" (David 2015: 10). Although machines are able to analyze data, they do not have intuition, cunning, adaptive intelligence or the ability to improvise (Karakilic 2022). Computers nowadays are still far away from having the level of intelligence of the average 5-year-old human (Petropoulos 2018). "Deep neural networks are still several orders of magnitude less complex than the human brain and closer to the computing power of a worm" (Petropoulos 2018: 123). Some scholars even doubt that artificial general intelligence will ever be developed (Gil et al. 2020). Although the emergence of Chat GPT caused some observers to wonder whether artificial general intelligence is closer at hand, this program seems not to have crossed that threshold. It draws on an extensive array of databases but still basically makes predictions based on its programming.

Robotics is another facet of the on-going technological revolution that is slowly changing the nature of work. Sales of these machines almost doubled between 2015 and 2016, reaching 10 million units sold per year. The decline in their cost enable some firms to deploy them even to replace low-cost laborers (West 2018). The share of the tasks performed by robots in manufacturers was roughly 10 percent in 2020. However, it is expected to reach 25 percent by 2025 (Fleming 2019). Nevertheless, the cost of integrating robots into assembly lines has been estimated to be three times as expensive as the robot itself (Autor et al. 2020). The overall cost of these machines could explain why two-thirds of them are being used primarily in machinery, metal, electrical, electronic and automobile industries (World Bank 2018). Roughly 40 percent of all robots are used in the automobile industry. Even in those industries in which they are currently being used, they are generally concentrated in certain parts of factory floors (Autor et al. 2020).

Smaller firms customarily augment their existing systems with new robots instead of installing entirely new ones, thereby minimizing disruptions for workers and limiting the need for terminations. However, many small firms do not introduce them simply because their small batch sizes do not permit the extensive standardization needed for them to be productive (Autor et al. 2020). Although robots are increasingly being used for activities outside the factory floor, they are still rather inflexible and clumsy compared to humans. For example, robots that unload trucks can only work with boxes with a relatively uniform size that are loaded in a specific fashion (Mims 2022). Robots also still prove ineffective in handling soft materials. As with AI, machines are replacing workers undertaking routine, standardized tasks. Humans remain critical in adapting work processes to changing conditions (Autor et al. 2020). Artificial intelligence and robots complement the work done by humans, rather than replacing it (Autor et al. 2020; David 2015). The real advantage of AI and robots lies in freeing up humans from doing tedious, repetitive work. For example, algorithms enable lawyers to avoid spending countless hours searching documents, enabling them to focus on the more analytical side of their work (Zamora 2020). Artificial intelligence proves less useful for industries that require counseling or extensive, direct interactions with clients (Vom Brocke et al. 2018). It can actually prove detrimental for companies operating in industries requiring constant innovations in products or production processes. It is not recommendable to use AI to make strategic decisions in companies because any choice made with it is likely to be similar to a company's competitors, thereby limiting the ability of a firm to differentiate itself (Birkinshaw 2020). In the end, new technological developments prove most effective for companies that produce standardize products in competitive environments that do not require extensive product adaptation or considerable changes in production processes.

5.2 Changes in the Nature of Jobs and Employment Schemes

Artificial Intelligence has not affected all workers equally. It has led to the displacement of those performing codifiable, routine, tasks such as repetitive production assignments, bookkeeping, and clerical work (Autor et al. 2020). New technological developments can enable businesses to lower prices, thereby potentially generating higher demand and even greater employment (Arntz et al. 2016). One example is the introduction of the automated teller machine. It enabled bank employees to focus more on building and maintaining relationships rather than performing basic tasks. Although it was commonly believed that these machines would lead to the elimination of jobs, the number of positions in this industry actually increased by roughly 10 percent from 1980 until 2010. The reduction in the number of tellers per branch was more than compensated by the fact that banks opened 40 percent more branches from 1988 to 2004 (Autor et al. 2020). Wages for workers can actually increase with the introduction of AI or robotics because it makes jobs faster, cheaper and more reliable (Haskel and Westlake 2017), thereby making workers more productive (Atkinson 2018) and raising the value of what they provide (David 2015). New technological developments can also change the nature of employment in an industry. Haskel and Westlake (2017) point out that Citibank now employs more programmers than Microsoft.

Employment has also been growing in low-skilled occupations that require dexterity (World Bank 2018). AI and robotics still cannot handle situations that are ambiguous, transient, or disorienting, because such tasks cannot be measured precisely or codified (Karakilic 2022). Although these technologies replace workers performing low-skill, repetitive tasks, they do not eliminate low-paid service jobs such as janitors, food service workers, landscapers, and security guards (Autor et al. 2020). These jobs are difficult to automate because they require judgment, flexibility, and common sense (David 2015). "While these activities are not highly skilled by the standards of the US labor market, they present daunting challenges for automation" (David 2015: 13). Workers with medium-level qualifications have more to fear from automation than those who have low-skilled jobs requiring judgment. Jobs that require creative and social skills as well as some degree of decision-making are less likely to be eliminated. They will continue to be in high demand for the foreseeable future (Petropoulos 2018; Schwab 2017).

Nevertheless, jobs are increasingly becoming more precarious. The emergence of crowdwork is just one example (Berg et al. 2018). People with these types of jobs are independent contractors located across the world that bid for individual tasks in a larger job, performing tasks that cannot be done by AI. These jobs involve responding to surveys, participating in experiments, classifying the quality of videos, collecting data, cleaning it, as well as categorizing, and tagging images. Roughly seventy million people work in this industry. This form of work emerged in the early 2000s when the Internet became more widely available across the globe (Woodcock and Graham 2019). Forty-eight percent of crowdworkers claimed that it was their only source of employment. On average workers spend 30 hours a week doing this type of work (O'Reilly et al. 2018). In 2017, they earned on average US$ 4.43 per hour. In the United States, crowdworkers earn less than the minimum wage of US$ 7.25. In Germany, 93 percent of workers on the Clickworker platform earn less than the minimum wage of €8.84 per hour. The average wages for crowdworkers is US$ 2.22 per hour in Asia and the Pacific and US$ 1.33 per hour in Africa (Berg et al. 2018). Seventy-two percent of crowdworkers have more than a high school diploma and one-fourth of them had technical certificates or some university experience. Thirty-seven percent had a bachelor's degree and twenty percent a postgraduate one. Nevertheless, "most microtasks are simple and repetitive and do not coincide with the high level of education of many crowdworkers" (Berg et al. 2018: xviii). In emerging markets highly educated people take these jobs because they sometimes pay more than any other job they can find (Berg et al. 2018).

During most of the twentieth century, the vast majority of workers in the developed world had full-time jobs in which pre-set schedules, benefits, and long-term tenures were the norm. By the end of that century, work was becoming more precarious with unpredictable schedules, fewer benefits and shorter tenures (Pilaar 2018). In those countries that have strong welfare states, the recent decline in full-time work is leading to a division in society in which people are being separated between those that work under the older norms and those that are employed under the new ones (Pilaar 2018). The latter do not have access to the welfare benefits enjoyed by the former (Berg et al. 2018). Yet, the introduction of new technologies does not naturally lead to an increase in the outsourcing of work. Indeed, it should lead to greater full-time employment. According to Coase (1937), firms hire employees instead of contractors for tasks that are complex and/or often change. These are exactly the tasks that AI and robots have difficulty performing.

According to Thelen (2019) technology per se is not the cause of the rise of precarious work. Instead, the way in which people are contracted depends on institutions. The growth in precarious work in the develop world is related more to changes in corporate policies and the unwillingness of governments to introduce new regulations. This style of contracting workers is not new. Although precarious work arrangements hark back to pre-industrial times in which people toiled in sweatshops (Berg et al. 2018), it also dominated employment in factories throughout the nineteenth century (Pilaar 2018). Like the precarious workers of today, neither these factory nor sweatshop workers had set schedules or any sense of permanence in their contractual relations. Many of the new precarious jobs are done by gig workers, namely people who take jobs on a short-term, temporary basis from a multiple of employers. They have no guarantee of finding new work once a job is complete, requiring them to often spend time without an income (Woodcock and Graham 2019). Gig workers tend to simultaneously hold several jobs (Johannessen 2018; World Bank 2018). Similar to cottage producers, these laborers often have to provide their own equipment.

5.3 The Impact of Institutional Frameworks on the Future of Work

Some countries are better positioned than others to take advantage of AI and robotics. Given that technologies diffuse relatively slowly, we should expect that countries in emerging markets will be less impacted by them than those in the developed world. Furthermore, I argue that the ability of firms operating in these countries to implement these new technological developments is also limited by difficulties they face in standardizing operations. This topic is discussed in detail in the subsection of this section on Brazil. I also contend that jobs in Germany will be less affected by AI and robotics because production in this country is not as standardized as countries such as the United States. At the same time, Germany has workers with the skills they need to use these new technological developments in a manner that augments their jobs rather than replacing them. The educational system is actually designed to provide workers these skills. By contrast, fewer workers in the United States have them and training in them is less widespread. Hence, companies are more likely to standardize more operations and terminate more workers. In the end, the potential impact of new technological developments on workplaces is shaped by socio-organizational factors. "It is not technology that determines employment patterns of organizational design but the other way around. The specific use of machinery is informed by socio-organizational forces" (Flemming 2019: 27). These factors can be at least partially understood by examining the five institutional variables of VoC. Now, I turn to an evaluation of the impact of these five variables on the implementation of new technological developments in the United States, Germany, and Brazil. They are prime examples of LMEs, CMEs, and HMEs, respectively.

5.3.1 United States

Although there are several countries that classify as LMEs, I will examine the United States because it is the prime example of this ideal type. Although orders for robots in this country rose from 30,000 per year in 2019 to 40,000 in 2021, it still ranked 7th in the world in robot density per worker. Nevertheless, the introduction of robotics and AI appears to have had a particularly strong impact on jobs there. Acemoglu and Restrepo (2019) argue that the income of workers in this country has been declining because alterations in production processes are not leading to new tasks for workers. In short, new technological developments are for the most part replacing workers rather than helping them complete tasks. At the same time, firms are increasingly turning toward more precarious forms of work. By 2010, contingent work in the United States came to represent 40 percent of all jobs (Pilaar 2018). "As of March 2019, Google had more temps and contractors than it did employees, even though the former work alongside the latter and sometimes do similar work" (Case and Deaton 2020: 238).

Even permanent workers are often treated like temporary ones in the United States. For example, Amazon has an average turnover rate in its full-time staff of 150 percent per year in its warehouses. This firm actually prefers that their employees in these facilities seek new jobs after having worked for them for roughly two years. In order to facilitate this rotation, Amazon relies on an extensive computer system to closely monitor its employees (New York Times 2021). AI proves valuable in overseeing workers conducting those tasks that still cannot be undertaken by robots. Nevertheless, employment in the warehouse industry in the United States is expected to grow by seven percent from 2020 until 2030 thanks to greater automation (Black 2022). Moreover, Walmart appears to be embracing an employment model that would complement the introduction of new technologies in the United States. In this country, this company raised the wages of 165,000 employees in September of 2020 as part of a process of creating new job categories that involved store clerks learning new skills so that they could easily move between tasks (Autor et al. 2020).

The five institutional spheres of VoC in the United States support standardization. In terms of governance, so finance, it is promoted by a short-term mentality that seeks to reduce costs by standardizing processes and products. This orientation also causes firms to hire unskilled workers as they are less expensive and can be easily replaced. Consequently, companies are also for the most part unwilling to invest in the skills of their workers. Their reluctance to do so is reinforced by the prevalence of poaching. Moreover, the educational system generally does not provide workers with the type of general skills they need to work in jobs that cannot be automated. This short-term, standardization mentality also drives the resistance firms generally have toward unionization. Companies simply view unions as a hindrance to greater standardization and attempts to implement technologies that could further standardize operations. Prakash (2023) points out that even companies such as Tesla and Starbucks have recently resisted the unionization of their workers. Employee relations are also short-term oriented. The weakness of labor laws limiting the ability of firms to terminate workers limits their ability to form committed relations with them, thereby further reinforcing standardization. In terms of inter-firm relations, companies prefer market relations because they are focused on reducing costs and are particularly well suited to providing them standardized inputs for their products.

5.3.2 Germany

This subsection focuses on Germany, as it is the quintessential CME. Technological developments are only having a moderate impact on the nature of work in this country (Rahner and Schönstein 2018), despite the fact that robot density per worker is one of the highest in the world (World Bank 2018). Production in Germany is characterized as having value chain processes that are not routine and designed to quickly adapt to the needs of customers. Companies generally produce a diversity of products in relatively small batches in the same facility (Sorge and Streeck 1988). Consequently, activities are less standardized and workers are needed to oversee the shift between different types of products. They also have to be able to resolve any problems that might occur in making these changes. Production processes are simply less standardized and, therefore, new technological developments have less of an impact on firms in this country than they do in LMEs like the United States.

Institutional investors continue to play only a minimal role in the system of governance in Germany. It remains dominated by large block holders that are generally interested in commitment and stability over the long term (Jackson and Thelen 2015). They are more concerned about long-term returns derived from investments in the batch production of quality goods than short-term gains made through the mass production of low-cost products through standardized procedures. The focus on long-term objectives is reinforced by supervisory boards that give employees voice in the operation of the firm (Hall and Soskice 2001). This type of co-participation is particularly well suited to diversified quality production. The mutual commitment between workers and firms is reinforced by a series of labor laws that shape the nature of employee relations in Germany. Labor laws place significant limitations on the ability of firms to terminate workers. Larger firms are even required to terminate young employees and send older ones into early retirement if they seek to undertake mass terminations. Nevertheless, these restrictions are counterbalanced by shared-work programs that enable companies to layoff workers for one day a week instead of firing them, thereby enabling firms to reduce the burden of labor costs without losing committed workers. Companies also have flexibility in deploying workers due to liberal regulations regarding overtime work. Although work hours are averaged over a week, any extra hours worked are put into an account. Within a six month period workers have to either take hours off in accord with the amount of extra time accumulated or be compensated for these hours at a higher rate; this period can be extended up to two years in collective bargaining agreements. It provides firms greater flexibility in deploying their workers and limiting the need to hire temporary ones (Friel 2003).

The training system in Germany emphasizes broad-based skills and problem-solving techniques (Friel 2005; 2003). These are exactly the skills that workers need to function effectively alongside robots and AI instead of being replaced by them. Thelen (2019) argues that this training system has become even more demanding of students over the past few years. The most significant problem in this system is the inability to incorporate more students. Hence, new entrants into the job market are increasingly being forced to take lower-skilled, lower paying jobs (Thelen 2012). Forty percent of the adult population in Europe have a higher level of skill than what is required for their current job (Atkinson 2018). Given this potential, it is not surprising that Antón et al. (2022) found that the impact of robots in Europe on job creation was positive from 2005 until 2015. Given the characteristics of the German employment system, we should not expect it to differ from other European countries in this regard. The relatively high level of skills of average workers in Germany enables firms also to work closely with their suppliers (Friel 2005, 2003). This attribute of supplier relations in Germany is particularly well suited to diversified quality production because firms need their suppliers to be able to quickly produce new components for their ever-changing products. Coase (1937) highlights that the market relations are good at producing standardized inputs. The ones needed by firms pursuing diversified quality production are not as standardized as those in the United States are. Therefore, the role of the traditional markets in governing supplier relations is less important in Germany.

5.3.3 Brazil

Brazil is the ideal case to examine the impact of AI and robotics on firms located in HMEs not only because it is the largest economy that currently belongs to this ideal type but also because it inspired the formation of it. I argue that new technological developments will not have a significant impact on the operations of firms in this country because they face a number of significant hurdles in standardizing their operations. They are distinct from the ones outlined for the German case above.

Schneider (2013) argues that political and economic instability in HMEs causes companies to rely principally on self-financing. In Brazil, there are only 345 companies listed on the stock exchange (World Bank 2016). Consequently, the capital they have to invest in new technological developments is limited. Although larger companies in Brazil can rely on the Brazilian Development Bank to help them finance the acquisition of new technologies (Pearson 2012), the vast majority of companies in this country tend to be smaller ones that lack access to these resources and have few funds available for self-financing (Maloney and Molina 2016). Consequently, they have difficulty purchasing new technologies. Even though robots have become less expensive recently, they are still prohibitively so for the overwhelming number of firms in Brazil. The lack of a developed infrastructure for installing and maintaining robots adds substantively to the cost of relying on them in emerging markets (Maloney and Molina 2016). There is no reason to expect that Brazil would differ from other countries in this category.

Even if a firm can afford these expenses, the nature of inter-firm relations in Brazil undermines their potential utility. As mentioned above, robotics only work well in situations in which parts are standardized (Autor et al. 2020). Yet, firms in emerging markets often face difficulties finding suppliers that can provide them with quality goods (Dunning and Lundan 2008; Teece 2014) because they face significant difficulties in absorbing technologies needed to make such inputs (Cuervo-Cazurra and Rui 2017). Lower quality goods are likely to have a wide variety of defects and imperfections. Consistency is the most significant problem in this regard. Elsewhere, I describe how an Argentine multinational in Brazil vertically integrated the production of some inputs to address problems of quality. For other inputs it trained the workers of its suppliers to make quality goods (Friel 2021). In short, the lack of quality and consistency in the inputs produced by suppliers of companies in Brazil limits their ability to implement new technological developments because they rely on goods being standardized with few defects. Hence, it is not the capacity of the firm per se but rather that of its suppliers that puts the greatest limitation on the ability of firms to standardize their operations.

Large firms and their suppliers are also limited in their ability to introduce new technological developments by their capability to absorb them, a workforce with the level of skills necessary to operate them, limited maintenance capacity and a low attention to tolerances (Maloney and Molina 2016). Although robots and AI can replace workers performing standardized processes, firms relying on these new technological developments still need relatively skilled workers to oversee them. People with such skills are difficult to find in Brazil. On average they have only 6.4 years of education (Aguzzoli and Geary 2014). By comparison, students in OECD countries receive 9.5 years of schooling on average (Vassolo, De Castro, Gomez-Mejia 2011). Roughly two-thirds of 15-year-old Brazilians were considered low achievers in math according to their scores on the PISA exam (Silva, Almeida, and Strokova 2015). The ability of firms to find appropriate workers is also hindered by the fact that forty percent of them are employed on the informal labor market in this country (Aguzzoli and Geary 2014). "In many developing countries many workers remain in low-productivity jobs, often in informal sectors with little access to technology" (World Bank 2018: 4). Again, there is no reason to believe that Brazil would differ from other emerging markets in this regard.

There is widespread agreement that employee relations in Brazil are hierarchical (Aguzzoli and Geary 2014; Bausch 2022; Schneider 2013). Relations between companies and their employees are paternalistic. Respect for hierarchy lies at the core of employee relations in this country. Decision-making is centralized and power distance is high. The importance of hierarchy is reflected in the fact that on average a manager earned five to seven times more than an employee (Bausch 2022). Paradoxically, the nature of labor laws in Brazil limits the ability of firms to develop long-term commitments with their employees. Wage earners are required to make monthly deposits of 8 percent of their salary into an escrow account. They can only access the funds in this account if they are fired, are older than seventy or use it to make a down payment on a house. The way in which indemnities are structured in Brazil serves to promote employee rotation because average workers do not have access to bank loans. Consequently, they often ask their employers to fire them so that they can tap into the funds in their escrow accounts (Friel and de Villechenon 2018). This behavior creates high turnover rates that limit commitment from employees and undermines the willingness of firms to train them. The ability of firms to form such bonds with their employees is further limited by the fact that outside the banking industry and the public sector unions in Brazil are weak and fragmented. In the areas in which they do exist, they are generally considered to be ineffective and focused almost exclusively on wages and working hours (Aguzzoli and Geary 2014). In the end, the implementation of AI and robotics in Brazilian firms is limited not only by their inability to find workers with the skills they need, but also by difficulties in retaining and empowering workers so that they could effectively work with these new technological developments.

5.3.4 Contrasting Policies across Ideal Types

In this chapter, I have demonstrated that the five institutions of VoC work to promote standardization in the United States and limit it in Germany and Brazil; see Table 2 for a summary of the impact of the five variables of VoC on standardization in each of these countries. I am not arguing that firms in either of these latter two countries standardize some operations. Indeed, for some processes AI and robots may prove effective in both Brazil and Germany. I simply argue that companies in these countries do not rely on these technologies as extensively as those in the United States. Therefore, new technological developments are likely to prove a greater threat to jobs in the United States than to those in Germany and Brazil.

6 Different Paths, Different Reforms

Hall and Soskice (2001) contend that their approach opens up a new perspective for a wide range of policy-related topics that shape the performance of an economy. It focuses attention on how improvements in the coordination of economic actors through institutions that channel their behavior in a particular direction can lead to better economic performance. They argue that "economic policies will be effective only if they are incentive compatible, namely complementary to the coordinating capacities embedded in the existing political economy" (Hall and Soskice 2001: 46). Institutional reforms prove effective only if they are compatible with existing incentive patterns for businesses (Jackson and Deeg 2006). One of the advantages of VoC is the fact that it views institutional change as being largely incremental and path-dependent (Jackson and Deeg 2006; Thelen 2012). The historical trajectory of a country places significant limits on how institutions can be altered (Hall and Taylor 1996). Research in this field has demonstrated that even after an extended period of time a substantial gap still exists between liberal and coordinated market economies. The way in which work is coordinated in an economy is not being altered (Hall and Thelen 2009). Even though economies across the globe

Table 2 VoC institutions and standardization in the United States, Germany, and Brazil.

	United States	Germany	Brazil
Governance	Short-term mentality supports standardization	Long-term focus not conducive to standardization	High cost of machines undermines automated standardization
Industrial Relations	Weak unions support standardization	The commitment of workers to the firm created by strong unions does not support standardization	Where unions do exist they only focus on wages and working hours, thereby promoting standardization
Vocational Training and Education	Unskilled workers with limited training support standardization	Training in broad-based skills does not support standardization	Lack of skills to operate new technological developments undermines automated standardization
Inter-firm Relations	Market relations focused on reducing costs support standardization	Close relationships with suppliers does not promote standardization	Lack of quality suppliers undermines automated standardization
Employee Relations	Ease of terminating workers supports standardization	Labor laws and shared-work programs support worker retention and undermine standardization	Hierarchical organizational structures and labor laws promoted employee rotation and standardization

are facing pressures ranging from the decentralization of collective bargaining to reductions in social benefits, they are not liberalizing or converging toward the LME ideal type (Hall and Thelen 2009). Even reforms in CMEs "rarely take the form of an outright dismantling of institutional support for coordination" (Jackson and Thelen 2015: 327). Any other type of change would undermine the increasing returns from the complementarities of existing institutions (Jackson and Deeg 2008a). Moreover, by couching institutional change in CMEs and HMEs in terms of liberalization, scholars overlook potential changes that are occurring even in LMEs.

As mentioned above, I argue that the nature of the five institutions in VoC in a given country shape the extent to which new technological developments will prove fruitful in it. Given that the United States has a relatively high degree of standardization and relatively few workers with the skills needed to work effectively with new developments, they are likely to displace a significant number of workers. Consequently, the government in this country will be under significant pressure to mitigate their impact on the lives of individuals that otherwise would end up in lower-paid service jobs or without any employment. The possibility that workers in Germany will face a similar fate is lower simply because these five institutions in this country support a lower degree of standardization. Therefore, AI and robots will have less impact on their operations and workers will not be as affected by them as in LMEs like the United States. Moreover, German workers are more likely to possess the skills necessary to obtain relatively good jobs working with these new technological developments. Although Brazil is more aligned with the United States than Germany in terms of the skills of its workforce, difficulties obtaining quality inputs makes the standardization required by AI and robots more difficult. While employee relations promote standardization, it is further limited by the nature of governance and industrial relations in this country. According to the World Bank (2018) more productivity gains in emerging markets in general could be achieved by improving the skills of workers, rather than by introducing new technological developments.

Palier (2018) suggests that governments have three broad ways of responding to challenges in the twenty-first century. They can introduce universal basic income (UBI), improve existing schemes for independent workers or implement flexicurity; flexicurity provides people "access to healthcare, housing, education and training, and a universal basic income without regard to employment status" (Palier 2018: 256). I suggest that the United States should implement a UBI program, while Germany should focus on flexicurity. Currently Brazil has a UBI program targeted at the poor. I argue that its government should expand the scope of this program to resemble flexicurity, albeit still focused only on the poor. To accomplish this task it would have to provide concrete benefits in terms of healthcare, housing, and education. I argue that the likelihood for the success of any reform in any country will depend on how well it is tailored to a nation's existing institutions. The changes any government undertakes should be informed by the ideal type to which it belongs, because reforms that don't fit existing institutional structures are likely to fail. Hence, I contend that governments can find appropriate examples from which they can learn by focusing on reforms undertaken by other countries that belong to their same ideal type. The rest of this section explores how successful reforms in the United States, Germany and Brazil could be undertaken in a way that takes the nature of the five institutions of VoC into consideration. As in the previous section, this one focuses on these countries because they are the quintessential representatives of LMEs, CMEs, and HMEs, respectively.

6.1 United States

The introduction of more sophisticated AI and robotics in the United States is leading a growing number of people that used to have middle-skilled jobs to be forced to take lower-paid, more precarious ones. White men without a four-year degree have been particularly disadvantaged. They saw their purchasing power decline by 13 percent from 1979 until 2017, even as national income over this same period grew by 85 percent (Case and Deaton 2020). Some of these displaced workers are simply dropping out of the labor force. The percentage of individuals in the United States between forty-five to fifty-four without a bachelor's degree that claimed they were unable to work grew from 4 percent in 1993 to 13 percent in 2017 (Case and Deaton 2020). The US government is reluctant to directly regulate the hiring practices of firms to help these displaced workers. However, I argue that political consensus could be formed around the creation of a UBI program. Politicians in the United States can draw on the widespread support for social security and the affordable care act to justify the implementation of a UBI program. According to Kalleberg (2018) the Affordable Care Act of 2010 was a move in the direction of UBI style benefits. Such policies are acceptable in the United States because they do not provide benefits to a limited group of people. By helping individuals cover some of their basic needs it would enable them to dedicate more of their own funds to obtaining the type of skills needed in societies in which AI and robotics play an increasing role.

Hall and Soskice (2001) contend "in general, liberal market economies should find it more feasible to implement market-incentive policies that do not put extensive demands on firms to form relational contracts with others but rely on markets to coordinate their activities. These include regional development schemes based on tax incentives" (49). In the United States, the national government offers a variety of tax benefits that help individuals with issues ranging from home ownership and health care to college attendance and retirement. The most effective way for the US government to shape governance is through tax policies. It could seek to limit the proliferation of precarious and poorly paid jobs simply by providing firms tax incentives to hire full-time workers at a living wage. This government could also use tax incentives to subsidize training programs within firms that lead to full-time, well-paid jobs. It could also further subsidize community colleges because these are the institutions that the poor largely rely on to improve their skills.

President Biden has voiced support for unions. A broad array of the US public shares his position. A Washington Post poll indicated that 71 percent of all people in the United States approved of them (Rosenfeld 2022). However, the United States is unlikely to shift toward the type of cooperative labor relations that exist in CMEs like Germany, despite the fact that they are exactly the type of labor relations needed in order for firms to embrace AI and robots without having a dramatic impact on employment. One significant hurdle to the realization of more cooperative relations between unions and firms in this country is that fact that such cooperation is explicitly prohibited by regulation 8(a)(2) of the National Labor Relations Board (Friel 2003). Although the national government is not acting to promote participatory relations between firms and unions, there are movements in this direction at the state level. One example of such a mechanism is recent legislation in California. The Fast Food Council in that state was authorized to establish an advisory group made up of four representatives from companies, four workers, and two state employees. They are charged with setting wages, working conditions and hours of work. The California legislature retains the prerogative to block any of the policies approved by this council (Ding and Hussain 2022). Some state and city governments also play an important role in actually promoting the operation of more efficient markets. They are forcing firms to be more transparent about pay. Since 2017 four states have adapted laws requiring employers to reveal salary ranges for new jobs. New York City has also passed a similar law for any company with over four employees (Goldberg and Kessler 2022). Although these types of laws at first glance would seem to be counter to the LME model, they are not because they facilitate the functioning of markets.

6.2 Germany

As mentioned above, German firms will be less impacted by AI and robotics than those in the United States. Nevertheless, the growing reliance on these new technological developments is further deepening the gap between insiders and outsiders. Workers with limited capabilities are facing increasing difficulties in finding jobs that provide them skills, union representation and relatively good wages. They are ending up in precarious jobs. Germany is now on par with liberal market economies such as Ireland and the United Kingdom in terms of the percentage of workers in low-paying jobs (Krings 2021). Germany has not followed the lead of some Nordic countries and the Netherlands to extend social benefits to part-time workers (Palier 2018). Moreover, it no longer provides welfare benefits to individuals that have so-called mini-jobs, namely short-term jobs that pay less than 520 euros per month, despite the fact that the proliferation of these jobs has contributed to the growth of the working poor in Germany (Johannessen 2018). This country is reducing its reliance on policies related to flexicurity when it should be strengthening them to offset the negative effects associated with the implementation of AI and robots. Improvements in such policies could be tolerated by business elites if the German government extended work-share programs and the period over which overtime hours have to be averaged. It could also limit the period over which firms can use temporary workers from two years to one year. These changes to existing laws would provide firms incentives to hire more permanent workers.

Although the institutional structures facilitating coordination between labor and management in the field of labor relations have been debilitated in Germany, they could be reinvigorated. Unions in this country would clearly be interested in increasing the number of full-time employees. They would also be interested in helping these workers improve their skills. Unions have traditionally pushed for workers to receive broad-based skills because it is a mechanism for them to more easily find better paying jobs (Lynch 1994). These are exactly the type of skills workers need to take full advantage of AI and robots. Although the apprenticeship system has been accommodating fewer and fewer students over the years (Thelen 2012), it could be reinvigorated to ensure workers had the skills needed. In order to entice more students and firms, the course of study could be simplified and the time it takes to learn a trade reduced. At the same time, apprenticeships may no longer be needed in some areas. They could be replaced with certificate programs from technical schools. This would reduce the burden on people to obtain skills, while also providing firms with more skilled workers. Relationships could also be deepened between firms in the area of inter-firm relations. Chambers of commerce in Germany are already involved in a variety of activities that facilitate coordination between firms. Hence, the German government could help them better coordinate their activities with their suppliers by providing funding for chambers of commerce targeted at helping companies implement AI and robotics.

6.3 Brazil

Given the dramatic differences between the United States and Brazil, the latter would not benefit from liberalization policies targeted at making it similar to the former. Indeed, as mentioned in Chapter 3, Schneider (2009) contends that the liberalization policies of the 1990s in Latin America did not alter the basic institutional structure of HMEs such as Brazil. Instead of implementing such policies, HMEs would be well advised to examine the reforms that are being undertaken by other countries that belong to their same ideal type. As mentioned above, countries like Brazil are unlikely to be dramatically impacted by new technological developments not only because it is difficult to standardize operations in these countries but also because technologies take more time to reach them. In this sense, the Brazilian government has more time to plan for the eventual impact that AI and robotics will have on its society. Any reforms undertaken by the Brazilian government should seek to stimulate the gradual incorporation of AI and robots into the operations of businesses, albeit perhaps in a manner that differs from how these technologies are being used in Germany and the United States. In the next chapter, I will discuss what type of production system may be best suited to Brazil and other HMEs. The most significant challenges facing Brazil in facilitating the creation of an effective employment system that can incorporate AI and robots are the reduction of precarious work, flexicurity programs for the poor, significant improvements in training institutions, and mechanisms to facilitate the purchase of AI and robots by small- and medium-sized companies.

Now, assistance to the poor in Brazil primarily comes from the Bolsa Família program. It is a UBI program that provides a basic cash transfer only to the poorest people in that country. It is the largest program of its kind in the world, reaching over 46 million people. It also provides the poor with contacts to complementary social services and jobs. This program could be extended to include job-related services that would help individuals with training and placement. It could also include bonuses for the participation of adults in continuing education and literacy programs (Lindert et al. 2007). In this sense, the Bolsa Família program would provide the basis for improving the skills of the poorest and move it in the direction of a flexicurity program. However, in order for Brazil to be able to embrace AI and robotics without negatively impacting most workers, it will also have to provide training programs at least to the lower middle-classes, if not to people in the middle class. This government could also seek to reinvigorate their training system in a manner similar to that recommended for Germany in the previous subsection. It could clearly define the type of skills workers need and focus on streamlining the training institutions that already exist to concentrate on these skills and reduce the time needed to receive certificates. Such a policy would provide more workers the training they need to function well with AI and robots. Unlike in Germany, the Brazilian government will face substantive difficulties in involving the unions that do exist in the training of workers as they are only interested in improving wages. Nonetheless, in those sectors in which unions are relatively strong in Brazil, the government could seek their help in reducing informal employment because it would increase their number of dues-paying members. According to the International Labor Organization (2015) over one-third of employed adults in Brazil work in the informal labor market. The Brazilian government should not seek to create new labor laws in order to try to incentivize firms to hire workers formally, simply because even existing labor laws are only enforced for larger firms where formal work already tends to dominate.

Loans from the Brazilian Development Bank could be used to promote a variety of policies. They prove particularly enticing because the interest rates charged are often substantively lower than loans made directly from banks (Friel 2011). The Brazilian government could have the Brazilian Development Bank make loans to small- and medium-sized companies that seek to improve the skills of their workers and use AI and/or robotics to improve their operations. It could also extend such loans to small- and medium-sized companies that want to invest in AI and robots as the lack of financial resources is the most important factor limiting the ability of these firms to buy these technologies. In helping these companies with such loans, the Brazilian government would also be addressing one of the most significant problems facing inter-firm relations and the implementation of new technological developments, namely the challenges of small- and medium-sized suppliers in providing their clients with higher quality inputs that would enable them to standardize their own operations. This government could also bolster formal employment by requiring firms to open their operations to inspections that would ensure workers are properly employed as a condition of receiving such loans, thereby reducing the main source of precarious work in this country. In this manner, the Brazilian government would be helping those companies that operate legally expand at the detriment to those that continue to function on the black market.

7 The Path Ahead for Work Using VoC

This Element demonstrates the utility of VoC in helping scholars and practitioners alike understand how a set of five critical variables shape the strategies and behaviors of firms above in beyond its original focus on comparative institutional advantages. It specifically analyzes how differences across these variables shape the future of work across countries, arguing that those countries with institutions that support standardization such as the United States will have a significantly greater number of individuals displaced from their jobs by AI and robots. Although some workers will also be displaced in countries with institutions that do not support the degree of standardization in LMEs like the United States, their numbers will not be as high. I argue that the impact of these new technological developments is mitigated in Germany by the fact that fewer tasks in diversified quality production in this country can be automated compared to mass production in the United States. I also contend that although forms of production in Brazil resemble mass standardized production, the difficulties faced by small- and medium-sized firms in financing the purchase of new technologies undermines standardization and their ability to replace workers with machines.

This Element also highlights the benefits of conducting fine-grained research on the five institutional variables of VoC across a greater variety of countries. I argue that more research needs to be done on these five variables in all of the ideal types discussed herein besides CMEs and HMEs. This research is essential not only for making effective comparisons between countries but also for understanding how these variables shape the strategies and behavior of firms. At the same time, new ideal types need to be created and underdeveloped ones reinvigorated so that work in VoC can cover more countries. Such work will enable countries to learn from other ones that belong to their same ideal type. I argue these ideas will proved more effective than those derived from the experiences of other countries because they will be more related to the nature of existing institutions. At the same time, more studies need to be done to document how institutions in LMEs shape firm behavior. For example, I have shown elsewhere how laws in the United States actually limit cooperation between workers and firms (Friel 2005, 2003). Although the national government may indeed have a less significant role in shaping institutions in LMEs like the United States, the role of state and local institutions may prove more important. Future work using VoC should explore how complementarities could potentially arise out of the five institutions of VoC at a variety of levels by building on the governance approach to examine state and local institutions. I have highlighted in the existing section how state and local laws can either hinder or facilitate more cooperative forms of coordination in the United States. Such work should also explore these five institutions at the four levels identified by Williamson (2000). In conducting research on the viability of a company in another country, scholars should also pay particular attention to informal institutions. As mentioned above, they exist in all five spheres in VoC. What remains unclear is how we can properly identify and compare them.

Until now, VoC has only described how comparative institutional advantages shape the type of innovation that is likely to occur within a given economy. Although it implicitly argues that mass standardization predominates in the United States and diversified quality production in Germany, this argument needs to be made more explicit with clear explanations of how the five institutions in this approach support different forms of production. At the same time, we need research to examine forms of production in other countries; here it is important to point out that with the term forms of production I am referring to forms of organizing all types of work, including services. We may find that other countries also have diversified quality production or mass standardized production. Although China is often described as having mass standardized production, the link between its institutions and this form of production is unclear. Nevertheless, we also need to be open to finding other forms of production. I coined the term non-standardized mass production to describe how things are made in Brazil. As described in Chapter 4, this type of production focuses on the creation of large quantities of goods, albeit in a non-standardized manner. It highlights the fact that it has a large degree of flexibility even while generally lacking the skills and suppliers needed to pursue the style of batch production undertaken in CMEs. If Brazil succeeds in reforming its institutions so that robots and AI can be introduced effectively into its businesses, I argue that, it could potentially move toward something I term as diversified medium-quality production, namely the production of a large variety of medium-quality products. Improvements in quality would derive from the introduction of new technologies. Any country that seeks to take advantage of the potential benefits of AI and robotics to improve the operations of businesses in a manner that will provide workers decent, well-paying jobs needs to focus on ensuring that they have the broad-based, analytical skills they need to fully take advantage of these new technological developments.

The VoC approach also has significant implications not only for how scholars conceive the nature of globalization but also how firms should choose the foreign countries into which they seek to expand their operations beyond merely selling the products they produce in their home country. Indeed, Hall and Soskice (2001) maintain that "comparative institutional advantages tend to render companies less mobile than theories that do not acknowledge them imply" (56). Although they do not elaborate on this statement, it would seem clear that companies would be well advised to work in countries that belong to the same ideal type as their home country, or at least in a country with a similar one. Comparative institutional advantages simply work better in countries that have similar institutional settings. Elsewhere, I have shown how the firm-specific advantages of companies from emerging markets are more suited to countries in the developing world than to those in the developed one (Friel 2021). Based on the analysis conducted in this Element, I would argue that firm-specific advantages of companies from an emerging market will only function well in other emerging markets that belong to the same ideal type as the company's host country. Hence, the development of more ideal types and the assignment of more countries to them, and to existing ones, would substantively help companies to be able to determine where they should open foreign operations.

Scholars could build on my previous work not only to include how past institutions could also play a role in forming complementarities, but also how firms could form their own comparative institutional advantages (Friel 2011). Such work would introduce more agency into the VoC framework, albeit in a way that preserves its focus on how the path dependency of institutions shapes firm behavior. In conducting such research scholars may indeed find that companies are creating similar comparative institutional advantages even in different countries. In undertaking such research they should keep in mind Whitley's (1999) contention that some countries may have more than one model of capitalism. Indeed, research using VoC may even find that the comparative institutional advantages in one region in a certain country are similar to that found in a region in a different nation. At the same time, scholars should not automatically assume that all countries have a comparative institutional advantage or that firms in a given country can actually form their own comparative advantage out of a variety of institutions. Such nations would indeed benefit in moving toward an ideal type. Yet, such a recommendation cannot be made until scholars have documented a wider variety of ideal types and connected them with clear comparative institutional advantages.

However, work using VoC should not be limited to only exploring comparative institutional advantages. This Element demonstrates that it can also prove useful in examining other topics. Future work could draw on it by exploring how the five institutions in this approach shape the ways in which governments can reduce climate change and mitigate its impact. It could also be used to examine reforms in health care and retirement systems. Although governments face similar problems, the way they address them will depend on the nature of the institutions identified in VoC. Work that is conducted on such topics using this approach should not only examine similarities between institutions in different countries but also how governments can learn from other countries that belong to their ideal type. In the end, the well-being of any country will be improved not by assuming that there is one right answer, but rather by understanding how each government can harness the power of its own institutions.

References

Acemoglu, D. and Restrepo, P. (2019). Automation and New Tasks: How Technology Displaces and Reinstates Labor. *Journal of Economic Perspectives*, 33(2), 3–30. http://doi.org/10.1257/jep.33.2.3.

Aguzzoli, R. and Geary, J. (2014). An "Emerging Challenge": The Employment Practices of a Brazilian Multinational Company in Canada. *Human Relations*, 67, 587–609. https://doi.org/10.1177/0018726713497523.

Albert, M. (1993). *Capitalism vs. Capitalism*. New York: Four Walls Eight Windows.

Allen, M. (2004). The Varieties of Capitalism Paradigm: Not Enough Variety? *Socio-Economic Review*, 2, 87–108. https://doi.org/10.1093/soceco/2.1.187.

Amable, B. (2003). *The Diversity of Modern Capitalism*. Oxford: Oxford University Press.

Antón, J. I., Klenert, D., Fernández-Macías, E., Urzì Brancati, M. C., and Alaveras, G. (2022). The Labour Market Impact of Robotisation in Europe. *European Journal of Industrial Relations*, 28(3), 317–39. https://doi.org/10.1177/09596801211070801.

Arnold, D., Arntz, M., Gregory, T., Steffes, S., and Zierahn, U. (2018). No Need for Automation Angst, but Automation Policies. In M. Neufeind, J. O'Reilly, and F. Ranft eds., *Work in the Digital Age: Challenges of the Fourth Industrial Revolution*, New York: Rowman and Littlefield, pp. 75–88.

Arntz, M., Gregory, T., and Zierahn, U. (2016). The Risk of Automation for Jobs in OECD Countries: A Comparative Analysis. *OECD Social, Employment and Migration Working Papers No. 189*. Paris: OECD. http://dx.doi.org/10.1787/5jlz9h56dvq7-enOECD.

Arthur, W. B. (1994). *Increasing Returns and Path Dependency in the Economy*. Ann Arbor: University of Michigan Press.

Arthur, W. B. (1989). Competing Technologies, Increasing Returns, and Lock-In by Historical Events. *The Economic Journal*, 99(394), 116–31. https://doi.org/10.2307/2234208.

Atkinson, R. (2018). Shaping Structural Change in the Era of New Technology. In M. Neufeind, J. O'Reilly, and F. Ranft eds., *Work in the Digital Age: Challenges of the Fourth Industrial Revolution*, London: Rowman and Littlefield International, pp. 104–16.

Autor, D, Mindell, D & Reynolds, E. (2020). *The Work of the Future: Building Better Jobs in an Age of Intelligent Machines*. MIT Industrial Performance Centre, Cambridge, accessed April 10, 2022. https://work

ofthefuture.mit.edu/research-post/the-work-of-the-future-building-better-jobs-in-an-age-of-intelligent-machines.

Baccaro, L. and Pontusson, J. (2018). Comparative Political Economy and Varieties of Macroeconomics. Max Planck Institute for the Study of Societies Discussion Paper No. 18/10, accessed December 1, 2021.

Baldwin, R. (2019). *The Globotics Upheaval: Globalization, Robotics, and the Future of Work*. Oxford: Oxford University Press.

Balliester, T. and Elsheikhi, A. (2018). The Future of Work: A Literature Review. ILO Research Department Working Paper No. 29, pp. 1–54, accessed April 7, 2022.

Bausch, M. (2022). *Intercultural Transfer of Management Practices of German MNC to Brazil: The Interplay of Translation and Recontextualization*. Wiesbaden: Springer Nature.

Becker, U. (2007). Open Systemness and Contested Reference Frames and Change: A Reformulation of the Varieties of Capitalism Theory. *Socio-Economic Review*, 5, 261–86. https://doi.org/10.1093/ser/mwl025.

Becker, U. (2013). Institutional Change in the BRICs, Eastern Europe, South Africa and Turkey, 1998–2008. In U. Becker ed., *The BRICs and Emerging Economies in Comparative Perspective: Political Economy, Liberalization and Institutional Change*, Abingdon: Routledge, pp. 27–52.

Becker, U. and Vasileva, A. (2017). Russia's Political Economy Re-conceptualised : A Changing Hybrid of Liberalism, Statism and Patrimonialism. *Journal of Eurasian Studies*, 8(1), 83–96. http://dx.doi.org/10.1016/j.euras.2016.11.003.

Benanav, A. (2020). Automation Isn't Wiping Out Jobs, It's that Our Engine of Growth Is Winding Down. The Guardian, January, 23. www.theguardian.com/commentisfree/2020/jan/23/robots-economy-growth-wages-jobs.

Berg, J., Furrer, M., Harmon, E., Rani, U., and Silberman, M. S. (2018). Digital Labour Platforms and the Future of Work. Towards Decent Work in the Online World. Report from the International Labor Organization, accessed April 6, 2022.

Birkinshaw, J. (2020). What Is the Value of Firms in an AI World? In J. Canals and F. Heukamp eds., *The Future of Management in an AI World: Redefining Purpose and Strategy in the Fourth Industrial Revolution*, London: Palgrave Macmillan, pp. 23–36.

Black, T. (2022). Bloomberg Robots Are Key to Winning the Productivity War. Bloomberg. August 19, accessed September 1, 2022. www.bloomberg.com/opinion/articles/2022-08-19/robots-are-key-to-winning-the-productivity-war.

Bohle, D. and Greskovitis, B. (2009). Varieties of Capitalism and Capitalism « tout court ». *European Journal of Sociology*, 50(3), 355–86. https://doi.org/10.1017/S0003975609990178.

Bohle, D. and Greskovits, B. (2012). *Capitalist Diversity on Europe's Periphery*. Ithaca: Cornell University Press.

Bruff, I., Ebenau, M., and May, C. (2015). Fault and Fracture? The Impact of New Directions in Comparative Capitalisms Research on the Wider Field. In M. Ebenau, I. Bruff, and C. May eds., *New Directions in Comparative Capitalisms Research: Critical and Global Perspectives*, London: Routledge, pp. 28–44.

Buhr, D. and Frankenberger, R. (2014). Emerging Varieties of Incorporated Capitalism. Theoretical Considerations and Empirical Evidence. *Business and Politics*, 16(3), 393–427. https://doi.org/10.1515/bap-2013-0020.

Cadena, A., White, O., and Lamanna, C. (2023). *Current Global Challenges Could Usher in a New Era*. What Might This Mean for Latin American Economies? McKinsey Global Institute. www.mckinsey.com/mgi/our-research/what-could-a-new-era-mean-for-latin-america.

Canals, J. (2020). The Evolving Role of General Managers in the Age of AI. In J. Canals and F. Heukamp eds., *The Future of Management in an AI World: Redefining Purpose and Strategy in the Fourth Industrial Revolution*, London: Palgrave Macmillan, pp. 37–66.

Case, A. and Deaton, A. (2020). *Deaths of Despair and the Future of Capitalism*. Princeton: Princeton University Press.

Chandler, A. D. (1977). *The Visible Hand: The Managerial Revolution in American Business*. Cambridge, MA: Belknap Press of Harvard University Press.

Chandy, L. (2017). The Future Work of in the Developing World: Brookings Blum Roundtable 2016 Post-Conference Report. www.brookings.edu/wp-content/uploads/2017/01/global_20170131_future-of-work.pdf.

Coase, R. (1937). The Nature of the Firm. Economica, 4, 386–405.

Coates, D. (2000). *Models of Capitalism: Growth and Stagnation in the Modern Era*. Cambridge: Polity Press.

Crouch, C. (2005). Models of Capitalism. *New Political Economy*, 10(4), 439–56. https://doi.org/10.1080/13563460500344336.

Crouch, C. and Farrell, H. (2002). *Breaking the Path of Institutional Development? Alternatives to the New Determinism*. European University Institute, Florence, Department of Political and Social Sciences No. 2002/4.

Crouch, C., Streeck, W., Boyer, R. et al. (2005). Dialogue on Institutional Complementarity and Political Economy. *Socio-Economic Review*, 2(4), 359–82. https://doi.org/10.1093/SER/mwi015.

Cuervo-Cazurra, A. and Rui, H. (2017). Barriers to Absorptive Capacity in Emerging Market Firms. *Journal of World Business*, 52(6), 727–42. https://doi.org/10.1016/j.jwb.2017.06.004.

Dallmayr, F. and McCarthy, T. (1977). Introduction: Max Weber and Verstehen. In F. Dallmayr and T. McCarthy eds., *Understanding and Social Inquiry*, London: University of Notre Dame Press, pp. 1–13.

David, P. (1985). Clio and the Economics of QWERTY. *American Economic Review*, 75(2), 332–37.

David, P. (1994). Why Are Institutions the "Carriers of History?": Path Dependence and the Organizations and Institutions. *Structural Change and Economic Dynamics*, 5(2), 205–20. https://doi.org/10.1016/0954-349X(94)90002-7.

David, H. (2015). Why Are There Still so Many Jobs? The History and Future of Workplace Automation. *Journal of Economic Perspectives*, 29(3), 3–30. https://doi.org/10.1257/jep.29.3.3.

Deeg, R. (2005). *Complementarity and Institutional Change: How Useful a Concept? Discussion Paper SP II 2005–21.* Berlin, Social Science Research Center Discussion Paper SP II.

Deeg, R. and Jackson, G. (2007). The State of the Art. Towards a More Dynamic Theory of Capitalist Variety. *Socio-Economic Review*, 5, 149–79. https://doi.org/10.1093/ser/mwl021.

Deeg, R., & Jackson, G. (2008). Comparing Capitalisms: Understanding Institutional Diversity and Its Implications for International Business. Journal of International Business Studies, 39(4), 540–61.

Ding, J. and Hussain, S. (2022). California Legislature Passes Bill to Protect Fast-Food Workers. Los Angeles Times, August 29, www.latimes.com/business/story/2022–08–09/california-senate-pass-bill-fast-food-workers, accessed October 5, 2022.

Dunning, J. and Lundan, S. (2008). *Multinational Enterprises and the Global Economy.* Northampton: Edward Elgar.

Ebenau, M. (2015). Directions and Debates in the Globalization of Comparative Capitalisms Research. In M. Ebenau, I. Bruff, and C. May eds., *New Directions in Comparative Capitalisms Research: Critical and Global Perspectives*, London: Routledge, pp. 45–64.

Ebenau, M., Bruff, I., and May, C. (2015). Introduction: Comparative Capitalisms Research and the Emergence of Critical, Global Perspectives. In M. Ebenau, I. Bruff, and C. May eds., *New Directions in Comparative Capitalisms Research: Critical and Global Perspectives*, London: Routledge, pp. 1–10.

Elmslie, B. and Criss, A. J. (1999). Theories of Convergence and Growth in the Classical Period: The Role of Science, Technology and Trade. *Economica*, 66(261), pp. 135–49. https://doi.org/10.1111/1468-0335.00160.

Feldmann, M. (2007). The Origins of Varieties of Capitalism: Lessons from Post-Socialist Transition in Estonia and Slovenia. In B. Hancké, M. Rhodes, and M. Thatcher eds., *Beyond Varieties of Capitalism*, Oxford: Oxford University Press, pp. 328–50.

Feldmann, M. (2019). Global Varieties of Capitalism. *World Politics*, 71(1), 162–96. https://doi.org/10.1017/S0043887118000230.

Fleming, P. (2019). Robots and Organization Studies: Why Robots Might Not Want to Steal Your Job. *Organization Studies*, 40(1), 23–37. https://doi.org/10.1177/0170840618765568.

Fligstein, N. and Freeland, R. (1995). Theoretical and Comparative Perspectives on Corporate Organization. *Annual Review of Sociology*, 21, 21–43. https://doi.org/10.1146/annurev.so.21.080195.000321.

Fligstein, N. and Zhang J. (2011). A New Agenda for Research on the Trajectory of Chinese Capitalism. *Management and Organization Review*, 7, 39–62. https://doi.org/10.1111/j.1740-8784.2009.00169.x.

Ford, M. (2018). The Rise of the Robots: Impact on Unemployment and Inequality. In E. Paus ed., *Confronting Dystopia: The New Technological Revolution and the Future of Work*. Ithaca: Cornell University Press, pp. 27–45.

Friedland, R. and Alford, R. (1991). Bringing Society Back in: Symbols, Practices, and Institutional Contradictions. In W. Powell and P. DiMaggio eds., *The New Institutionalism in Organizational Analysis*, Chicago: University of Chicago Press, pp. 232–64.

Friel, D. (2003). Labor Policy, Choice, and the Organization of Work: A Case Study of the Efficacy of Lean Production at a German Conglomerate in the United States and Germany, unpublished Doctoral dissertation, New School for Social Research.

Friel, D. (2005). Transferring a Lean Production Concept from Germany to the United States: The Impact of Labor Laws and Training Systems. *Academy of Management Perspectives*, 19, 50–58. https://doi.org/10.5465/ame.2005.16962752.

Friel, D. (2011). Forging a Comparative Institutional Advantage in Argentina: Implications for Theory and Praxis. *Human Relations*, 64(4), 553–72. https://doi.org/10.1177/0018726710396244.

Friel, D. (2021). Breaking the Looking Glass: Understanding How Emerging Market Multinationals Develop Unique Firm-specific Advantages. *Journal of International Management*, 27(3). https://doi.org/10.1016/j.intman.2021.100831.

Friel, D. and de Villechenon, F. (2018). Adapting a Lean Production Program to National Institutions in Latin America: Danone in Argentina and Brazil. *Journal of International Management*, 24(3), 284–99. https://doi.org/10.1016/j.intman.2018.03.001.

Friel, D. and Teipen, C. (2000). Corporate Reorganization in Germany and the United States: Institutional Challenges and Opportunities. Unpublished Paper Presented at Economics and Politics of Labor in Advanced Societies, Berlin, June.

Garg, P. (2023). The Future of Consulting in the Age of Generative AI. EY. www.ey.com/en_in/consulting/the-future-of-consulting-in-the-age-of-gen erative-ai.

Giddens, A. (1984). *The Constitution of Society: Outline of the Theory of Structuration*. Cambridge, MA: Polity Press.

Gil, D., Hobson, S., Mojsilović, A., Puri, R., and Smith, J. (2020). AI for Management: An Overview. In J. Canals and F. Heukamp eds., *The Future of Management in an AI World: Redefining Purpose and Strategy in the Fourth Industrial Revolution*, London: Palgrave Macmillan, pp. 3–22.

Goldberg, E. and Kessler, S. (2022). New Laws Force Honesty about Pay. Companies Are Catching Up. New York Times, October 29, www.nytimes .com/2022/10/29/business/nyc-us-salary-transparency.html, accessed April 22, 2022.

Granovetter, M. (1985). Economic Action and Social Structure: The Problem of Embeddedness. *American Journal of Sociology*, 91, 481–510. https://doi.org/ 10.1086/228311.

Hall, P. (1999). The Political Economy of Europe in an Era of Interdependence. In H. Kitschelt, P. Lange, G. Marks, and J. Stephens eds., *Continuity and Change in Contemporary Capitalism*, New York: Cambridge University Press, pp. 135–63.

Hall, P. (2015). Varieties of Capitalism. In R. Scott, S. Kosslyn, and N. Pinkerton eds., *Emerging Trends in the Social and Behavioral Sciences: An Interdisciplinary, Searchable, and Linkable Resource*, New York: John Wiley & Sons, pp. 1–15.

Hall, P. and Gingerich, D. (2009). Varieties of Capitalism and Institutional Complementarities in the Political Economy: An Empirical Analysis. *British Journal of Political Science*, 39, 449–82. https://doi.org/10.1017/ S0007123409000672.

Hall, P. and Soskice, D. (2001). Introduction. In P. Hall and D. Soskice eds., *Varieties of Capitalism: The Institutional Foundations of Comparative Advantage*, London: Oxford University Press, pp. 1–68.

Hall, P. and Taylor, R. (1996). Political Science and the Three New Institutionalisms. *Political Studies*, 44, 936–57. https://doi.org/10.1111/ j.1467-9248.1996.tb00343.x.

Hall, P. and Thelen, K. (2009). Institutional Change in Varieties of Capitalism. *Socio-Economic Review*, 7, 7–34. https://doi.org/10.1093/ser/mwn020.

Hancké, B., Rhodes, M., and Thatcher, M. (2007). Introduction: Beyond Varieties of Capitalism. In B. Hancke, M. Rhodes, and M. Thatcher eds., *Beyond Varieties of Capitalism: Conflict, Contradictions, and Complementarities in the European Economy*, New York: Oxford University Press, pp. 223–52.

Haskel, J. and Westlake, S. (2017). *Capitalism without Capital*. Princeton: Princeton University Press.

Hay, C. (2020). Does Capitalism (Still) Come in Varieties? *Review of International Political Economy*, 27(2), 302–19. https://doi.org/10.1080/09692290.2019.1633382.

Hertog, S. (2022). Segmented Market Economies in the Arab World: The Political Economy of Insider–Outsider Divisions. *Socio-Economic Review*, 20(3), 1211–47. https://doi.org/10.1093/ser/mwaa016.

Herrigel, G. (1996). *Industrial Constructions: The Sources of German Industrial Power*. Cambridge: Cambridge University Press.

Hollingsworth, J. and Streeck, W. (1994). Countries and Sectors. In J. R. Hollingsworth, P. C. Schmitter, and W. Streeck eds., *Governing Capitalist Economies: Performance and Control of Economic Sectors*, New York: Oxford University Press, pp. 270–300.

Hotho, J. and Saka-Helmhout, A. (2017). In and between Societies: Reconnecting Comparative Institutionalism and Organization Theory. *Organization Studies*, 38(5), 647–66. https://doi.org/10.1177/0170840616655832.

International Labor Organization. (2015). Informal Employment among Youth in Brazil. www.ilo.org/wcmsp5/groups/public/–ed_emp/–ed_emp_msu/documents/publication/wcms_542021.pdf.

Jackson, G. and Deeg, R. (2006). How Many Varieties of Capitalism? Comparing the Comparative Institutional Analyses of Capitalist Diversity. Discussion Paper. Max Planck Institute for the Study of Societies, Cologne, June.

Jackson, G. and Deeg, R. (2008a). Comparing Capitalisms: Understanding Institutional Diversity and Its Implications for International Business. *Journal of International Business Studies*, 39, 540–61. https://doi.org/10.1057/palgrave.jibs.8400375.

Jackson, G. and Deeg, R. (2008b). From Comparing Capitalisms to the Politics of Institutional Change. *Review of International Political Economy*, 15(4), 680–709. https://doi.org/10.1080/09692290802260704.

Jackson, G. and Deeg R. (2012). The Long-Term Trajectories of Institutional Change in European Capitalism. *Journal of European Public Policy*, 19(8), 1109–25. https://doi.org/10.1080/13501763.2012.709001.

Jackson, G. and Deeg, R. (2019). Comparing Capitalisms and Taking Institutional Context Seriously. *Journal of International Business Studies*, 50, 4–19. https://doi.org/10.1057/s41267-018-0206-0.

Jackson, G., Helfen, M., Kaplan, R., Kirsch, A., and Lohmeyer, N. (2019). The Problem of De-Con- Textualization in Organization and Management Research. In T. B. Zilber, J. M. Amis, and J. Mair eds., *The Production of Managerial Knowledge and Organizational Theory: New Approaches to Writing, Producing and Consuming Theory*. Bingley: Emerald, pp. 21–42.

Jackson, G. and Thelen, K. (2015). Stability and Change in CMEs: Corporate Governance and Industrial Relations in Germany and Denmark. In P. Beramendi, S. Häusermann, H. Kitschelt, and H. Kriesi eds., *The Politics of Advanced Capitalism*, Cambridge: Cambridge University Press, pp. 305–31.

Johannessen, J. A. (2018). *The Workplace of the Future: The Fourth Industrial Revolution, the Precariat and the Death of Hierarchies*. New York: CRC Press.

Kalleberg, A. (2018). US Balancing Risks and Improving Job Quality in a Changing Economy. In M. Neufeind, J. O'Reilly, and F. Ranft eds., *Work in the Digital Age: Challenges of the Fourth Industrial Revolution*, London: Rowman and Littlefield International, pp. 513–26.

Karakilic, E. (2022). Why Do Humans Remain Central to the Knowledge Work in the Age of Robots? Marx's Fragment on Machines and Beyond. *Work, Employment and Society*, 36(1), 179–89. https://doi.org/10.1177/0950017020958901.

Khanna, T. and Palepu, K. (1997). Why Focused Strategies May Be Wrong for Emerging Markets. *Harvard Business Review*, 75, 41–48.

Khanna, T. and Palepu, K. (2010). *Winning in Emerging Markets: A Road Map for Strategy and Execution*. Boston: Harvard Business Press.

King, P. (2007). Central European Capitalism in Comparative Perspective. In B. Hancke, M. Rhodes, and M. Thatcher eds., *Beyond Varieties of Capitalism: Conflict, Contradictions, and Complementarities in the European Economy*, Oxford: Oxford University Press, pp. 307–27.

Kıran, J. (2018). Expanding the Framework of the Varieties of Capitalism: Turkey as a Hierarchical Market Economy. *Journal of Eurasian Studies*, 9, 42–51. https://doi.org/10.1016/j.euras.2017.12.004.

Krings, T. (2021). 'Good' Bad Jobs? The Evolution of Migrant Low-Wage Employment in Germany (1985–2015). *Work, Employment and Society*, 35(3), 527–44. https://doi.org/10.1177/0950017020946567.

Lewin, A.Y. and Kim, J. (2004). The Nation State and Culture as Influences on Organizational Change and Innovation. In M. S. Poole and A. H. Van de Ven eds., *Handbook of Organizational Change and Innovation*, Oxford: Oxford University Press, pp. 324–53.

Lindert, K., Linder, A., Hobbs, J., and De la Brière, B. (2007). The Nuts and Bolts of Brazil's Bolsa Família Program: Implementing Conditional Cash

Transfers in a Decentralized Context. World Bank Social Protection Discussion Paper No. 709.

Locke, R. (1995). *Remaking the Italian Economy*. Ithaca and London: Cornell University Press.

Loveday, M. and Brady, K. (2023). Germany's Far-Right Party is More Popular than Ever – and More Extreme. Washington Post. August 21, www.washing tonpost.com/world/2023/08/18/germany-afd-polls-krah/#

Lynch, L. (1994). Payoffs to Alternative Training Strategies at Work. In R. Freeman, ed., *Working under Different Rules*, New York: Russell Sage Foundation

Maira, J. and Martib, I. (2009). Entrepreneurship in and around Institutional Voids: A Case Study from Bangladesh. *Journal of Business Venturing*, 24(5), 419–35. https://doi.org/10.1016/j.jbusvent.2008.04.006.

Mahoney, J. and Thelen, K. (2010). A Theory of Gradual Institutional Change. In J. Mahoney and K. Thelen eds., *Explaining Institutional Change: Ambiguity, Agency and Power*, Cambridge: Cambridge University Press, pp. 1–37.

Malone, T. (2020). How Can Human-Computer "Superminds" Develop Business Strategies? In J. Canals and F. Heukamp eds., *The Future of Management in an AI World: Redefining Purpose and Strategy in the Fourth Industrial Revolution*, London: Palgrave Macmillan, pp. 165–84.

Maloney, W. F. and Molina, C. (2016). Are Automation and Trade Polarizing Developing Country Labor Markets, Too? World Bank Policy Research Working Paper No. 7922.

McCarthy, N. (2020). Where People Are Losing Faith in Capitalism. Forbes, January 23. www.forbes.com/sites/niallmccarthy/2020/01/23/where-people-are-losing-faith-in-capitalism-infographic/?sh=594f774d7493.

Mims, C. (2022). Meet the army of robots coming to fill in for scarce workers. Wall Street Journal. October 15, www.wsj.com/articles/meet-the-army-of-robots-coming-to-fill-in-for-scarce-workers-11665806451?mod=mhp.

Molina, O. and Rhodes, M. (2007). The Political Economy of Adjustment in Mixed Market Economies: A Study of Spain and Italy. In B. Hancke, M. Rhodes, and M. Thatcher eds., *Beyond Varieties of Capitalism: Conflict, Contradictions, and Complementarities in the European Economy*, New York: Oxford University Press, pp. 223–52.

Morgan, G., Doering, H., and Gomes, M. (2021). Extending Varieties of Capitalism to Emerging Economies: What Can We Learn from Brazil? *New Political Economy*, 26(4), 540–53.https://doi.org/10.1080/13563467 .2020.1807485.

Musacchio, A. and Lazzarini, S. (2014). *Reinventing State Capitalism: Leviathan in Business, Brazil and Beyond*. Boston: Harvard University Press.

Myant, M. and Drahokoupil, J. (2012). International Integration, Varieties of Capitalism and Resilience to Crisis in Transition Economies. *Europe-Asia Studies*, 64(1), 1–33. https://doi.org/10.1080/09668136.2012.635478.

New York Times. (2021). Inside Amazon's Employment Machine. New York Times, January 15, 2021, www.nytimes.com/interactive/2021/06/15/us/amazon-workers.html, accessed August 15, 2022

Nölke, A. and Claar, S. (2013). Varieties of Capitalism in Emerging Economies. *Transformation*, 81/82, 33–54. http://doi.org/10.1353/trn.2013.0001.

Nölke, A., ten Brink, T., Claar, S., and May, C. (2015). Domestic Structures, Foreign Economic Policies and Global Economic Order: Implications from the Rise of Large Emerging Economies. *European Journal of International Relations*, 21(3), 538–67. http://doi.org/10.1177/1354066114553682.

Nölke, A., ten Brink, T., May, C., and Claar, S. (2020). *State-permeated Capitalism in Large Emerging Economies*. London: Routledge.

Nölke, A. and Vliegenthart, A. (2009). Enlarging the Varieties of Capitalism: The Emergence of Dependent Market Economies in East Central Europe. *World Politics*, 61(4), 670–702. http://doi.org/10.1017/S0043887109990098.

North, D. (1990). *Institutions, Institutional Change and Economic Performance*. Cambridge: Cambridge University Press.

Nübler, I. (2018). New Technologies, Innovation, and the Future of Jobs. In E. Paus ed., *Confronting Dystopia: The New Technological Revolution and the Future of Work*, Ithaca: Cornell University Press, pp. 46–75.

Oppenheimer, A. (2019). *The Robots are Coming!: The Future of Jobs in the Age of Automation*. New York: Vintage.

O'Reilly, J., Ranft, F., and Neufeind, M. (2018). Introduction: Identifying the Challenges for Work in the Digital Age. In M. Neufeind, J. O'Reilly, and F. Ranft eds., *Work in the Digital Age: Challenges of the Fourth Industrial Revolution*, London: Rowman and Littlefield International, pp. 1–24

Palier, B. (2018). The Politics of Social Risks and Social Protection in Digitalised Economies. In M. Neufeind, J. O'Reilly, and F. Ranft eds., *Work in the Digital Age: Challenges of the Fourth Industrial Revolution*, London: Rowman and Littlefield International, pp. 247–58.

Paul, D. (1994). Why Are Institutions the Carriers of History?: Path Dependence and the Evolution of Conventions, Organizations and Institutions. *Structural Change and Economic Dynamics*, 5(2), 1–24. https://doi.org/10.1016/0954-349X(94)90002-7.

Paus, E. (2018). The Future Isn't What It Used to Be. In E. Paus ed., *Confronting Dystopia: The New Technological Revolution and the Future of Work*. Ithaca: Cornell University Press.

Peck, J. and Theodore, N. (2007). Variegated Capitalism. *Progress in Human Geography*, 31(6), 731–72. https://doi.org/10.1177/0309132507083505.

Peck, J. and Zhang, J. (2013). A Variety of Capitalism ... with Chinese Characteristics? *Journal of Economic Geography*, 13(3), 357–96, https://doi.org/10.1093/jeg/lbs058.

Pearson, S. (2012). Brazil: A Bank Too Big to be Beautiful. Financial Times (September 23). www.ft.com/content/983f1bca-0234-11e2-b41f-00144feabdc0.

Petropoulos, G. (2018). The Impact of Artificial Intelligence on Employment. In M. Neufeind, J. O'Reilly, and F. Ranft eds., *Work in the Digital Age: Challenges of the Fourth Industrial Revolution*, London: Rowman and Littlefield International, pp. 119–32.

Pilaar, J. (2018). Assessing the Gig Economy in Comparative Perspective: How Platform Work Challenges the French and American Legal Orders. *Journal of Law and Policy*, 27, 47.

Polanyi, K. (2001). *The Great Transformation*. Boston: Beacon Press

Powell W. and DiMaggio, P. (1991). Introduction. In W. Powell and P. DiMaggio eds., *The New Institutionalism in Organizational Analysis*, Chicago: University of Chicago Press, pp. 1–38.

Prakash, P. (2023). Tesla Workers Trying to Unionize Are Turning to the Group that Launched Starbucks' Nationwide Union Wave. Fortune. February 15, https://fortune.com/2023/02/15/workers-united-union-starbucks-organize-tesla-employees-unionize-elon-musk/.

Rahner, S. and Schönstein, M. (2018). Germany: Rebalancing the Coordinated Market Economy in Times of Disruptive Technologies. In M. Neufeind, J. O'Reilly, and F. Ranft eds., *Work in the Digital Age: Challenges of the Fourth Industrial Revolution*, London: Rowman and Littlefield International, pp. 371–84.

Regini, M. (1997). Social Institutions and Production Structure: The Italian Variety of Capitalism in the 1980s. In C. Crouch and W. Streeck eds., *Political Economy of Modern Capitalism: Mapping Convergence and Diversity*, London: Sage Publications, pp. 102–16.

Rosenfeld, J. (2022). *Why Labor Unions Are More Popular than They've been in Six Decades*, Washington Post, September 5, www.washingtonpost.com/politics/2022/09/05/labor-unions-unionization-us/.

Sabel, C. and Zeitlin, J. 1997. Stories, Strategies, Structures: Rethinking Historical Alternatives to Mass Production. In C. Sabel and J. Zeitlin eds., *World of Possibilities: Flexibility and Mass Production in Western Industrialization*, New York: Cambridge University Press, pp. 1–33.

Šćepanović, V. and Bohle, D. (2018). The Institutional Embeddedness of Transnational Corporations: Dependent Capitalism in Central and Eastern

Europe. In A. Nölke and C. May eds., *Handbook of the International Political Economy of the Corporation*, London: Edward Elgar, pp. 152–66.

Schedelik, M., Nölke, A., Mertens, D., and May, C. (2021). Comparative Capitalism, Growth Models and Emerging Markets: The Development of the Field. *New Political Economy*, 26(4), 514–26. https://doi.org/10.1080/13563467.2020.1807487.

Schlumberger, O. (2008). Structural Reform, Economic Order, and Development: Patrimonial Capitalism. *Review of International Political Economy*, 15(4), 622–49. https://doi.org/10.1080/09692290802260670.

Schmidt, V. (2003). French Capitalism Transformed, Yet Still a Third Variety of Capitalism. *Economy and Society*, 32(4), 526–54. https://doi.org/10.1080/0308514032000141693.

Schmidt, V. (2010). Give Peace a Chance: Reconciling Four (Not Three) New Institutionalisms. In D. Béland and R. Cox eds., *Ideas and Politics in Social Science Research*, Oxford: Oxford University Press, pp. 64–89.

Schneiberg, M. (2007). What's on the Path? Path Dependence, Organizational Diversity and the Problem of Institutional Change in the US Economy, 1900–1950. *Socio Economic Review*, 5, 47–80. https://doi.org/10.1093/ser/mwl006.

Schneider, B. (2009). Hierarchical Market Economies and Varieties of Capitalism in Latin America. *Journal of Latin American Studies*, 41, 553–75. https://doi.org/10.1017/S0022216X09990186.

Schneider, B. (2013). *Hierarchical Capitalism in Latin America: Business, Labor, and the Challenges of Equitable Development*. Cambridge: Cambridge University Press.

Schwab, K. (2017). *The Fourth Industrial Revolution*. New York: Crown Business.

Silva, J. Almeida, R., and Strokova, V. (2015). Sustaining Employment and Wage Gains in Brazil: A Skills and Jobs Agenda. World Bank. http://hdl.handle.net/10986/22545. License: CC BY 3.0 IGO.

Smith, A. (1776). *The Wealth of Nations / Adam Smith; Edited, with Introduction, Notes, Marginal Summary, and Index by Edwin Cannan*. New York: Modern Library, 2000.

Smith, N. (2023). Nobody Knows How Many Jobs Will "Be Automated." https://policycommons.net/artifacts/3531658/nobody-knows-how-many-jobs-will-be-automated/4332647/.

Sorge, A. and Streeck, W. (1988). Industrial Relations and Technical Change: The Case for an Extended Perspective. In R. Hyman and W. Streeck eds., *New Technology and Industrial Relations*, Oxford: Blackwell, pp. 19–44.

Sorge, A. and Streeck, W. (2018). Diversified Quality Production Revisited: Its Contribution to German Socio-Economic Performance Over Time. *Socio-Economic Review*, 16(3), 587–612. https://doi.org/10.1093/ser/mwy022.

Soskice, D. (1999). Divergent Production Regimes: Coordinated and Uncoordinated Market Economies in the 1980s and 1990s. In H. Kitschelt, P. Lange, G. Marks and J. Stephens eds., *Continuity and Change in Contemporary Capitalism*, New York: Cambridge University Press, 101–34.

Stark, D. (1996). Recombinant Property in East European Capitalism. *The American Journal of Sociology*, 101(4), 993–1027.

Storz, C. Amable, B. Casper, S., and Lechevalier, S. (2013). Bringing Asia into the Comparative Capitalism Perspective. *Socio-Economic Review*, 11, 217–32. https://doi.org/10.1093/ser/mwt004.

Streeck, W. (1991). *On the Institutional Conditions of Diversified Quality Production*. In E. Matzner and W. Streeck eds., Beyond Keynesianism, Aldershot: Edward Elgar, pp. 21–61.

Streeck, W. (1996). Lean production in the German Automobile Industry: A Test Case for Convergence Theory. In S. Berger and R. Dore eds., *National Diversity and Global Capitalism*, Ithaca: Cornell University Press, pp. 138–70.

Streeck, W. (1997). German Capitalism: Does It Exist? Can It Survive? In C. Crouch and W. Streeck eds., *Political Economy of Modern Capitalism: Mapping Convergence and Diversity*, London: Sage Publications, pp. 237–56.

Streeck, W. (2001). Introduction: Explorations into the Origins of Nonliberal Capitalism in Germany and Japan. In W. Streeck and K. Yamamura eds., *The Origins of Nonliberal Capitalism: Germany and Japan in Comparison*, Ithaca: Cornell University Press, pp. 1–38.

Streeck, W. (2010). E pluribus unum? Varieties and Commonalities of Capitalism, Max Plank Institute for the Study of Societies Discussion Paper No. 10/12.

Streeck, W. and Thelen, K. (2005). Introduction: Institutional Change in Advanced Political Economies. In W. Streeck and K. Thelen eds., *Beyond Continuity*. Oxford: Oxford University Press, pp. 1–38.

Streeck, W. and Yamamura, K. (2003). Introduction: Convergence or Diversity? Stability and Change in German and Japanese Capitalism. In W. Streeck and K. Yamamura eds., *The End of Diversity? Prospects for German and Japanese Capitalism*, Ithaca: Cornell University Press, 1–50.

Sydow, J. Schreyögg, G., and Koch, J. (2009). Organizational Path Dependence: Opening the Black Box. *Academy of Management Review*, 34, 689–709. https://doi.org/10.5465/amr.34.4.zok689.

Sydow, J. and Windeler, A. (2020). Temporary Organizing and Permanent Contexts. *Current Sociology*, 68(4), 480–98. https://doi.org/10.1177/0011392120907629.

Tate, J. (2001). National Varieties of Standardization. In P. Hall and D. Soskice eds., *Varieties of Capitalism: The Institutional Foundations of Comparative Advantage*, London: Oxford University Press, pp. 442–73.

Teece, D. (2014). A Dynamic Capabilities-Based Entrepreneurial Theory of the Multinational Enterprise. *Journal of International Business Studies*, 45(1), 8–37. https://doi.org/10.1057/jibs.2013.54.

The Economist Group. (2022). Seizing the Opportunity: The Future of AI in Latin America. https://impact.economist.com/perspectives/sites/default/files/seizing-the-opportunity-the-future-of-ai-in-latin-america.pdf.

Thelen, K. (2001). Varieties of Labor Politics in the Developed Democracies. In P. Hall and D. Soskice eds., *Varieties of Capitalism: The Institutional Foundations of Comparative Advantage*, London: Oxford University Press, pp. 1–68.

Thelen, K. (2004). *How Institutions Evolve: The Political Economy of Skills in Germany, Britain, the United States and Japan*. New York: Cambridge University Press.

Thelen, K. (2012). Varieties of Capitalism: Trajectories of Liberalization and the New Politics of Social Solidarity. *Annual Review of Political Science*, 15, 137–59. https://doi.org/10.1146/annurev-polisci-070110-122959.

Thelen, K. (2019). Transitions to the Knowledge Economy in Germany, Sweden, and the Netherlands. *Comparative Politics*, 51(2), 295–315. https://doi.org/10.5129/001041519X15647434969821.

Thelen, K. and Steinmo, S. (1992). Historical Institutionalism in Comparative Politics. In S. Steinmo, K. Thelen, and F. Longstreth eds., *Structuring Politics: Historical Institutionalism in Comparative Perspective*, Cambridge: Cambridge University Press, 1–32.

Turner, L. (1991). *Democracy at Work: Changing World Markets and the Future of Labor Unions*. Ithaca: Cornell University Press.

Vassolo, R., De Castro, J., and Gomez-Mejia, L. (2011). Managing in Latin America: Common Issues and a Research Agenda. *Perspectives*, 25(4), 22–36. https://doi.org/10.5465/amp.2011.0129.

Viebrock, E. and Clasen, J. (2009). Flexicurity and Welfare Reform: A Review. *Socio-Economic Review*, 7(2), 305–31. https://doi.org/10.1093/ser/mwp001.

Vom Brocke, J., Maaß, W., Buxmann, P. et al., (2018). Future Work and Enterprise Systems. *Business and Information Systems Engineering*, 60(4), 357–66. https://doi.org/10.1007/s12599-018-0544-2.

Wehr, I. (2015). Entangled Modernity and the Study of Variegated Capitalism: Some Suggestions for a Postcolonial Research Agenda. In M. Ebenau, I. Bruff, and C. May eds., *New Directions in Comparative Capitalisms Research: Critical and Global Perspectives*, London: Routledge, pp. 134–54.

West, D. M. (2018). *The Future of Work: Robots, AI, and Automation.* Washington, DC: Brookings Institution Press.

Whitley, R. (1999). *Divergent Capitalisms: The Social Structuring and Change of Business Systems.* Oxford: Oxford University Press.

Williamson, O. (2000). The New Institutional Economics: Taking Stock, Looking Ahead. *Journal of Economic Literature*, 38(3), 595–613. https://doi.org/10.1257/jel.38.3.595.

Witt, M. A. and Jackson, G. (2016). Varieties of Capitalism and Institutional Comparative Advantage: A Test and Reinterpretation. *Journal of International Business Studies*, 47, 778–806. https://doi.org/10.1057/s41267-016-0001-8.

Witt, M. A., Kabbach de Castro, L. R., Amaeshi, K. et al. (2018). Mapping the Business Systems of 61 Major Economies: A Taxonomy and Implications for Varieties of Capitalism and Business Systems Research. *Socio-economic Review*, 16(1), 5–38. https://doi.org/10.1093/ser/mwx012.

Witt, M. A. and Redding, G. (2013). Asian Business Systems: Institutional Comparison, Clusters and Implications for Varieties of Capitalism and Business Systems Theory. *Socio-Economic Review*, 11(2), 265–300. https://doi.org/10.1093/ser/mwt002.

Witt, M. A. and Redding, G. (2014). Authoritarian Capitalism. In M. Witt, and G. Redding eds., *The Oxford Handbook of Asian Business Systems*, Oxford: Oxford University Press, pp. 26–51.

Wolf, M. 2023. *The Crisis of Democratic Capitalism.* New York: Penguin Press.

Wood, G. and Schnyder, G. (2021): Intro: Comparative Capitalism Research in Emerging Markets – A New Generation. *New Political Economy*, 26(4), 509–13. https://doi.org/10.1080/13563467.2020.1807488.

Woodcock, J. and Graham, M. (2019). *The Gig Economy: A Critical Introduction.* Cambridge, MA: Polity.

World Bank. (2018). World development report 2019: The changing nature of work. www.worldbank.org/en/publication/wdr2019.

World Bank. (2016). Listed domestic companies, total. http://data.worldbank.org/indicator/CM.MKT.LDOM.NO.

Zamora, J. (2020). Managing AI within a Digital Density Framework. In J. Canals and F. Heukamp eds., *The Future of Management in an AI World: Redefining Purpose and Strategy in the Fourth Industrial Revolution*, London: Palgrave Macmillan, pp. 205–35.

Cambridge Elements ≡

Reinventing Capitalism

Arie Y. Lewin

Duke University

Arie Y. Lewin is Professor Emeritus of Strategy and International Business at Duke University, Fuqua School of Business. He is an Elected Fellow of the Academy of International Business and a Recipient of the Academy of Management inaugural Joanne Martin Trailblazer Award. Previously, he was Editor-in-Chief of *Management and Organization Review* (2015–2021) and the *Journal of International Business Studies* (2000–2007), founding Editor-in-Chief of *Organization Science* (1989–2007), and Convener of Organization Science Winter Conference (1990–2012). His research centers on studies of organizations' adaptation as co-evolutionary systems, the emergence of new organizational forms, and adaptive capabilities of innovating and imitating organizations. His current research focuses on de-globalization and decoupling, the Fourth Industrial Revolution, and the renewal of capitalism.

Till Talaulicar

University of Erfurt

Till Talaulicar holds the Chair of Organization and Management at the University of Erfurt where he is also the Dean of the Faculty of Economics, Law and Social Sciences. His main research expertise is in the areas of corporate governance and the responsibilities of the corporate sector in modern societies. Professor Talaulicar is Editor-in-Chief of Corporate Governance: An International Review, Senior Editor of Management and Organization Review and serves on the Editorial Board of Organization Science. Moreover, he has been Founding Member and Chairperson of the Board of the International Corporate Governance Society (2014–2020).

Editorial Advisory Board

About the Series

This series seeks to feature explorations about the crisis of legitimacy facing capitalism today, including the increasing income and wealth gap, the decline of the middle class, threats to employment due to globalization and digitalization, undermined trust in institutions, discrimination against minorities, global poverty and pollution. Being grounded in a business and management perspective, the series incorporates contributions from multiple disciplines on the causes of the current crisis and potential solutions to renew capitalism.

Panmure House is the final and only remaining home of Adam Smith, Scottish philosopher and 'Father of modern economics.' Smith occupied the House between 1778 and 1790, during which time he completed the final editions of his master works: The Theory of Moral Sentiments and The Wealth of Nations. Other great luminaries and thinkers of the Scottish Enlightenment visited Smith regularly at the House across this period. Their mission is to provide a world-class 21st-century centre for social and economic debate and research, convening in the name of Adam Smith to effect positive change and forge global, future-focussed networks.

ADAM SMITH
PANMURE
HOUSE

Cambridge Elements ≡

Reinventing Capitalism

Printed in the United States
by Baker & Taylor Publisher Services